Due North of Montana

Due North of Montana

A Guide to Flyfishing in Alberta

Chris Dawson

Johnson Books
BOULDER

Spring Creek Press
ESTES PARK

Published in the United States by Johnson Books, a Division of Johnson Publishing Company, 1880 South 57th Court, Boulder, Colorado 80301.

9 8 7 6 5 4 3 2 1

Cover design: Margaret Donharl
Photographs: Chris Dawson

Library of Congress Cataloging-in-Publication Data
Dawson, Chris.
    Due north of Montana : a guide to flyfishing in Alberta / Chris Dawson.
        p.   cm.
    Includes index.
    ISBN 1-55566-180-7 (alk. paper)
    1. Trout fishing—Alberta—Guidebooks. 2. Fly fishing—Alberta—Guidebooks. 3. Rivers—Alberta—Guidebooks. 4. Alberta—Guidebooks. I. Title.
    SH688.C2D38   1996
    799.1'755—dc20   96-31156
                                                                                                      CIP

Printed in the United States by
Johnson Printing
1880 South 57th Court
Boulder, Colorado 80301

 Printed on recycled paper with soy ink

for

James, Carole, and Wally—

the rest of
the gang

Contents

Preface

I remember a time, not that long ago, when anglers equated Alberta flyfishing with the Bow River. Americans and other visiting flyrodders would show up in Calgary, fish the heck out of the Bow for a few days, then pack their bags. If a guide suggested that, "Hey, there are a lot of *other* good rivers here as well, you know," the client would usually hem and haw a bit and make a beeline straight for the airport and the next stop on the itinerary.

Well, times have changed. The Bow is still one of the best trout streams in the world, but foreign anglers are discovering what we Albertans have known all along—this province is a relatively untrammeled flyfishing paradise. There are gurgling spring creeks meandering past weathered barns, and there are boisterous freestone rivers cutting notches in the eastern slopes of the Rocky Mountains. The variety of water is, quite simply, overwhelming.

So is the variety of fish. Rainbows, browns, cutthroats, goldens, Arctic grayling—Alberta has them all. If your cravings tend more toward pike, whitefish, or goldeye, there are lots of those around, too. In fact, one thing that's always puzzled me is why Montana is lauded as flyfishing's mecca while Alberta goes relatively unnoticed. A quick glance at any map will show that they abut one another. The forty-ninth parallel separating the United States and Canada is a political contrivance that has nothing whatsoever to do with fishing quality.

When it comes to Alberta and Montana, the differences in climate and geography are slight; the differences in fishing pressure and public access are vast. It's also worth noting that the whirling disease that has devastated Montana fisheries like the Madison and Ruby Rivers has yet to surface in Alberta. We can only hope it stays that way.

Not that long ago I came across a magazine article on flyfishing in Montana by American writer Charles Gaines. In it he writes: "Like them or not, rod fees are a permanent feature on the new face of Western trout fishing. Ten years ago, you could knock on a rancher's door and get permission to fish almost any water that ran through private land. Now the state's blue-ribbon trout water, particularly that with no public access, is as valuable as oil."

I'll let you in on a little secret: rod fees are almost unheard of in Alberta. Most ranchers here will still give you permission to fish if you ask politely. I used to make twice-yearly pilgrimages to Montana, but now I'm just as content to stay in Alberta. Part of the reason is better access, to be sure, but to be honest, I catch just as many fish on my home waters as well. There are still trout streams in Alberta where I can fish on a weekend without seeing another angler; there are still tailwaters where the fish outnumber the flyfishers. This book reveals some of those spots.

It's always difficult to write a where-to book without upsetting people: I'm sure I'll have a few enemies when all is said and done. So be it. My self-imposed rule is this: I won't mention a river by name unless it's already well-known or someone is commercially guiding on it. After all, fair's fair. I also make no apologies for limiting the rivers in this book to southern Alberta (and one in southern British Columbia). The rationale is twofold: first, that's where the best trout fishing is; and second, those are the rivers most accessible to visiting anglers.

Where appropriate, I've tried to work some popular lakes into the text as well. One of the rivers featured, the Elk, is actually located in southeastern British Columbia. I've included it here because, for better or worse, the Elk has been appropriated by southern Albertans due to its proximity to the provincial border and to the popular Crowsnest River. I've also divided the Bow into its upper (above Calgary) and lower (below Calgary) sections. The nature of the fishing changes dramatically as the Bow leaves the foothills and enters the prairies; to deal with the entire river inclusively would have done both the reader and the Bow a disservice.

Each chapter consists of two distinct sections. The first provides a narrative, chronicling the flyfishing, people, geography, history, and "sense of place," that sets the stage for part two—how to find and fish the damn thing! I've called this latter section "When You Go," and it should provide all the specific information you'll need to successfully flyfish the river.

Finally, as you'll quickly gather, I'm definitely rooted in the "presentationist" flyfishing camp. The choice of a fly pattern is as personal as the choice of a mate. I wouldn't try to push a husband or wife on you, and I won't try to tell you to use a size 12 Bent-Hackle Reverse-Tied mayfly imitation if a size 12 Adams will do just fine.

Hopefully, this book will lead you to an Alberta river or two and serve as a starting point. That's my job—to lead you to the trestle bridge and the water's edge and to recommend a fly or two and let you know where you can get a good dinner at the end of the day. Whether you head upstream or down is entirely up to you.

Acknowledgments

Above all I wish to thank the guides and fishing companions whose expertise and generosity made this book possible. Most of them are mentioned in the text, but I'd also like to acknowledge Greg Cullen and Paul Bach. The number of other people I'm indebted to exceed the space allotted here, but I'd especially like to thank Fiona Kirkpatrick for the wonderful maps; my mother and father, who ignored the squirrels outside the window long enough to proofread the copy and provide invaluable guidance; editors Scott and Julie Roederer of Spring Creek Press; and publisher Barbara Mussil of Johnson Books, who continues to believe a Canadian has something worthwhile to say about flyfishing, eh.

Most of all, I wish to thank my wife, Christine Clarke—friend, lover, confidante, editor, and sometimes fishing partner. My passion for flyfishing is great, but it pales in comparison to my passion for her.

"When in the presence of natural order,
we remember the potentiality of life,
which has been overgrown by civilization."
—Terry Tempest Williams,
An Unspoken Hunger

Introduction

I've made enough road trips to Montana and other states to know there are certain logistical details that have to be taken care of before you can start fishing. With that in mind, the following advice should ease your transition from crossing the international border, to crossing the river in order to reach that rising trout along the far bank.

When to Come

Although springtime flyfishing can be quite good in Alberta (see the "Seasons and Tactics" heading in each chapter for specific details), the ideal time to come is from late June to early October. Most of the rivers in this book drain mountainous terrain that receives ample snowfall each winter, and spring run-off generally lasts from mid-May to late June, muddying the rivers and rendering them unfishable. There are, however, notable exceptions, such as the fabulous June dry-fly fishing on the Crowsnest and North Raven rivers.

By July, the other rivers and creeks will be clear as well (barring heavy rains), and this is a prime flyfishing month in southern Alberta, with good hatches of mayflies, caddisflies, and stoneflies. Superb grasshopper and caddis fishing extends through August and into September, when small blue-winged olive mayflies attract the attention of flyrodders and fish. Alberta often gets a lengthy dose of Indian summer in early October, and the blue sky, yellow leaves, and crystalline water combine to make autumn my favorite flyfishing season.

What to Bring

One word sums up the Alberta weather: changeable. Conditions are especially unpredictable during the spring and early summer. Typically, the skies are clear in the morning, with clouds rolling eastward off the mountains as the day progresses. Late afternoon thundershowers are common. The weather tends to stabilize by mid-July, and August and September are typically quite dry, particularly the farther east you travel from the mountains. Visiting anglers should bring everything from rain gear to sunglasses, from shorts to fleece jackets.

For flyfishing equipment, you'll also want both chest and hip waders, sturdy wading boots with felt soles, and a net with an opening large enough to land big fish. A nine-foot, six-weight rod is an ideal all-round choice; a second rod would be a four-weight for the smaller rivers and creeks. Don't forget floating, sink-tip, and sinking fly lines. Leaders should vary in length from seven-and-a-half to twelve feet, tippets from 1X to 6X. As for flies, see the "Fly Patterns" listing in each chapter for specific information. If you're buying flies, I'd recommend doing it when you get here.

Dealing with Customs

Whether you drive, fly, or paddle a canoe into Canada, legally you're required to tell a customs officer how long you intend to stay in the country and what the nature of your visit is. A typical response would be, "One week and to flyfish." Above all, be truthful and let the official know your plans. You'll also need reliable ID, such as a driver's license or American passport. Still, don't fret it. Border crossings by American anglers into Canada are routine, though you should still check with a local U.S. customs office regarding any liquor, tobacco, or firearm restrictions. Generally, you are not allowed to bring firearms or other self-defense weapons into Canada.

Passengers on all U.S. flights into Canada must clear customs at the airport. If you're driving north from Montana, there are three major border crossings: Coutts (open 24 hours, seven days a week); Carway (open daily from 8 A.M. to 11 P.M.); and Roosville (also open 24 hours daily).

Fishing Licenses and Information

Alberta angling licenses are available from most fly shops and sporting goods stores, and you can also find them at a number of gas stations and hardware stores throughout the province. Non-resident licenses cost about $27 (American) per season, which begins April 1 and runs until the following March 31. A five-day license is also available for about $18. If you're planning to fish the upper Bow River in Banff National Park (or waters in any other national park, for that matter), you'll need a park pass and fishing license. A daily pass is $4 per person ($7.50 for a group); a license is $4.50 per week or $10 per season. Because it's in British Columbia, anglers fishing the Elk River must purchase a B.C. freshwater license. For more information, see the "Special Regulations" heading in the Elk River chapter.

Anglers trailing their own driftboats or rafts to Alberta should note that vehicle shuttles are readily available at some rivers and non-existent at others. For example, while you won't have any trouble arranging a shuttle along the lower Bow, the same service is hard to come by on the upper river. The best bet is to check with the nearest fly shop or outfitter, because most of the shuttle services book through the shops anyway. (See the "Guides and Outfitters" heading in each chapter.) The detailed chapter maps include put-ins and take-outs on rivers large enough to float.

Flyfishers should also note that the Alberta government publishes a couple of useful travel planners and vacation guides. For copies of current editions and a provincial highway map, write to: Commerce Place Building, 10155 102nd St., Edmonton, Alta., Canada, T5J 4L6; telephone 800-272-9675 or 403-427-4321 in-province.

River Access

In Alberta, anglers have unlimited access to any river or lake in a national park or provincial forest reserve, provided the water is open to fishing (check the sportfishing regulations supplied with your license). Rivers flowing across private or leased land are a different story. The law stipulates that anglers fishing on private land must stay below the high-water mark, which is usually the maximum distance the water rises along the banks each spring during run-off. As a result, unless the banks are overgrown, steeply cut, or otherwise impeded, it's often possible to walk along the water's edge without trespassing. Nevertheless, if there's any doubt in my mind, I always ask the landowner for permission.

Alberta ranchers and farmers are still quite tolerant of flyfishers, and my experience is that you'll rarely be turned away. Every once in awhile you'll come across a section of river with wooden stiles (small stepladders or gates) crossing the barbed-wire fences on private or leased land (there are quite a few along the Highwood River gorge off Secondary Highway 541). The stiles are provided by landowners and permit anglers access to the river. Use respect when crossing private land. The stiles are often accompanied by a posted notice to that effect, but when unsure about a landowner's intent, I prefer to err on the side of caution and formally seek permission.

Like many fishing destinations, some of the best places to access Alberta's streams and rivers are at bridge crossings, campgrounds, and other public sites along the water. Unlike other destinations, there's still some surprisingly good flyfishing close to these access points. In fact, some of my most productive fishing has occurred within eyesight of blacktop bridges, so don't feel compelled to wear the felt off your wading boots hiking ten miles up every piece of water you come across. Alberta's rivers, including those listed in this book, still receive scant angling pressure compared to those in most parts of the States.

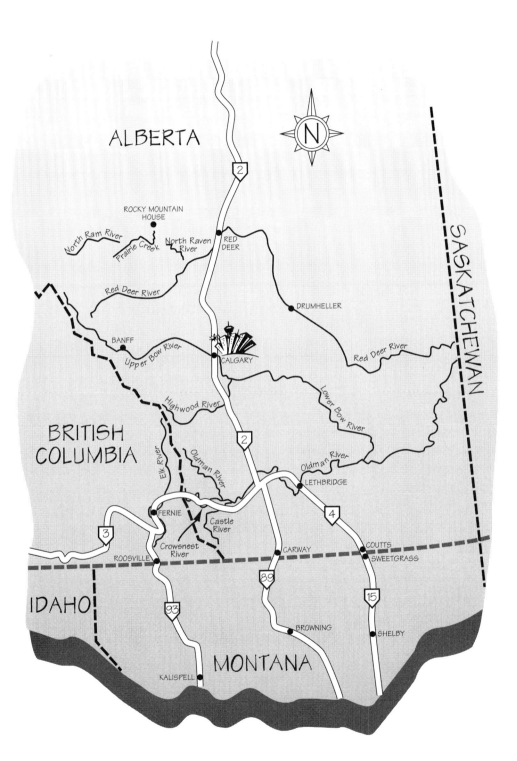

Part One

Calgary Area

1
Lower Bow River

It usually begins when dusk envelops the river, inky and warm; when the first fluttering caddisfly lodges itself between your cheek and your eyeglasses; when the first riseform, subtle as a leaf alighting on the water's surface, appears on the darkening current.

Most flyrodders have long since packed their rods and driven home. You wade as a blind man walks—tentative, probing, feeling, listening. The gravel shifts and settles beneath your felt-soled boots, the tug of the current is amplified by the onset of night. Before long the riseforms increase in number, the only physical sign that links you to the nether region where huge brown and rainbow trout hover beneath the surface. The caddisflies also increase in number as the hatch peaks. You pick them out of your ears and remove your glasses to wipe them away from your eyes. In the last remaining light, you can see the caddisflies swarming over your hands and arms, mistaking them, perhaps, for the security of tree limbs. You work some line out, casting blindly. You strip in line and stare at the spot on the water where the fly *should* be, because by now it's too dark to see something as inconspicuous as a quarter-inch tuft of elk hair. A fish rises in the vicinity—a gulp more audible than visible—and you set the hook, just in case. There is resistance, and then all hell breaks loose as the fish streaks away.

"Welcome," you tell yourself, stumbling along the bank after the trout, "to the Bow River caddisfly hatch in August. It doesn't get any better than this."

Or does it? What about the March brown hatch in May? The pale morning dun hatch in July? The blue-winged olive hatch in September?

One of the things I like best about the lower Bow (that section flowing southeast out of Calgary for about fifty miles to the Carseland weir) is the infinite variety of fishing it offers. Commonly, you'll find yourself casting nymphs in the morning, streamers in the afternoon, and dry flies in the evening. Or just the opposite. Ultimately, the fish will let you know what's working and what's not. Therein lies the secret to successful flyfishing on the Bow—adaptability.

The lower Bow is a large, meandering trout stream, characterized by stagnant backwaters and braided channels that wind through a broad valley of towering cottonwoods and stunted willows. For the most part the river is at least several hundred feet wide.

Often are the times I've come across a visiting angler on the bank, asked him or her how it's going, and been told something along the lines of, "It isn't. I just can't figure this thing out." I usually reply by telling the person to think of the Bow as the sum of many smaller parts. In other words, seek out the channels and fish them the same way you'd fish the familiar small creek back home. Bow River rainbows and browns prefer the same lies as other trout— eddies, deflections, underwater structure, and slack water along the banks. One of these days I'm going to photocopy an excerpt from a Russell Chatham essay and start handing it out to perplexed flyfishers.

"No matter what the water, you never just fish anywhere you want, but fishing a big river isn't as restrictive or intimidating as it first appears," Chatham writes in the compelling book *Dark Waters*. "It's simply a matter of learning to find those places where the river will allow you to fish. Each different river tells you in its own way. All you have to do is listen."

*   *   *

Ian Thomson's wife is pretty good about his fishing, but sometimes, as he's piling gear into his green Mackenzie drift boat with a go-cup full of coffee on the gunwale, she tries to place some limits to our adventures.

"You have to be back by seven," Lisa told him before a recent outing. "We have plans tonight." I don't know why, but she always looks at *me* when laying down the ground rules, as if *I'm* the one who controls our destiny. I was tempted to remind her that I was just along for the ride and that Ian is the one who named his boat *The Other Woman*, but the keys were in the ignition, the truck running, and you don't risk aborting the launch when all systems are go. I kept my mouth shut.

Ian has been flyfishing for about five years now, and he's taken to it. He's a thirtysomething Dan Quayle look-alike, all grin and charisma with a political pedigree courtesy of his father, a former member of the Canadian parliament. Unlike Quayle, Ian is perceptive—his potatoes in a row. He, too, kept his mouth shut until we'd pulled out of the driveway.

"Do you really think we'll be back by seven?" I asked.

"I doubt it."

It was mid-July—prime time. The lower Bow fishing season generally gets underway by April (discounting the insane few who thrash the water all winter), but angling then can be sporadic. The trout, still lethargic, are bunched up in deep pools. Most flyfishers dredge the bottom with heavily-weighted nymphs or streamers, but some get lucky and stumble across trout rising to midges. Run-off varies according to the mountain snowpack and spring rain, but it usually begins sometime in early June and lasts until the end of the month.

You want to be on the river as soon as the cloudy water starts clearing and dropping in late June. You want to be lobbing Woolly Buggers and Clouser Minnows tight to the banks, because by that time the big rainbows and browns will be holding there, behind boulders, sunken logs, and beaver houses. You want to cast slightly downstream from the drifting boat, giving the floating line a quick upstream mend. That creates a belly in the line, preventing it from being tugged downstream by the faster current between you and the bank, and allows the weighted streamer to sink a few feet. Often you can see it from the boat, its purple or black marabou tail dancing beneath the surface. Then you want to strip line as fast as you can, yanking the streamer into the faster water. If you're lucky, a silver or amber flash will follow—a flash as precise as a cruise missile flying through Saddam Hussein's window. The fish will smash the streamer, in an attempt to cripple it, and then take the hook in its mouth. Because this is the Bow River, there is a very good chance the trout will be twenty inches or longer. Most of the time it will measure between fourteen and eighteen inches.

But on this particular day in mid-July, Ian and I didn't intend to fish streamers. As we backed the drift boat into the river under the Highway 22X bridge in southeast Calgary, we both took four-weight, dry-fly rods out of their cases. Oh, sure, we rigged a streamer rod as well, but only as insurance—a second-string quarterback to bring off the drift boat bench if the dry flies sputtered. Our intended quarry were the big trout supposedly eating pale morning dun mayflies in shallow water. A friend had told me about them a day earlier in a fly shop; Ian had heard pretty much the same thing via a different grapevine. When Norman Maclean wrote, in *A River Runs Through It*, that eventually "all things merge into one," he could easily have been describing the convergence that takes place when flyfishers hear rumor of a major hatch on a river.

In the case of the lower Bow, the midday PMD hatch is the one that elevated the river from local hot spot to international destination. During the late 1970s and early 1980s, angling celebrities like A.J. McClane, Charles Brooks, and Lefty Kreh began to praise the Bow as one of the best dry-fly streams in the world. The magazines took notice, of course, and the convergence was under way.

I'm always amazed at the impact a magazine article can have on a trout stream. When *Fly Fisherman* printed a piece on southern Alberta's Crowsnest River complete with beautiful photographs, a buddy of mine who runs a bed-and-breakfast down there said his phone rang off the hook for weeks.

Anyway, Ian and I finished loading the boat and headed downstream, looking for "snouts" in the sparkling green current. This is a wonderful stretch of river. Mule deer abound in the sharply-cut coulees leading down to the water from the fields of wheat and barley above the valley's rim. Coyotes yelp and howl at dawn and dusk; porcupines, skunks, and beavers wander among stands of cottonwoods and white spruce at the river's edge. The honking of Canada geese is incessant, and the cackling of cock pheasants lasts well into the summer. Flocks of pelicans ride spiraling air currents on wings as wide as rafts, while

On the lower Bow, there's always a good chance for a rainbow over twenty inches.

red-tailed hawks and golden eagles search for rodents scurrying through the prairie grass. You'd be hard-pressed to convince an angler new to the river that cresting the valley would bring the Calgary skyline clearly into view.

The fishing was slow to begin with, and we anchored the boat through a stretch called the Thousand Islands where Ian worked a San Juan Worm below a gravel riffle. I worked a nearby raspberry patch in the middle of an island, fighting my way through the thorny tangle while stuffing myself with fuzzy red fruit. A lone great blue heron eyed me dubiously.

"Are you here to fish or to eat?" Ian asked disgustedly.

"I'm having better luck than you are," I replied.

We hopped back in the boat and continued downstream. Ian's boat, you should understand, is a limousine with oars. Among the extras he's built into its wooden frame are: a thermometer, drink holders, fancy storage cabinets, and Velcro rod holders. When we reached a particularly flat and serene stretch called Must-Be-Nice, we finally found what we were looking for. Four or five big fish, holding in the tail of a pool in less than a foot of water, were sipping PMDs from the surface. As we approached the trout from downstream, along the bank, every now and then we'd see a palm-sized tail or dorsal break the surface, wriggle enticingly, and then disappear. At such times I can't help but think of Captain Ahab, the lunatic whaler who lost his ship and his life in the single-minded pursuit of Moby Dick. Ahab, I've often thought, would have made a great flyfisher, swapping his harpoon for a Sage.

I took first crack at the pod. I tied on a size 16 Borger Yarn Wing Dun, my favorite PMD imitation, and carefully waded into the water about thirty feet behind the nearest fish. Because the current picked up speed just in front of me where it coursed over the pool's tail, I knew I'd have to throw some slack into the leader to give the fly time to float over the trout before the faster water tugged the line downstream.

It took several passes to hook a fish, including one in which I pulled the fly out of a trout's mouth while Ian guffawed from the bank. Hooking a big trout in "thin" water is a bit like flushing a pheasant in the waist-high grass—sheer commotion. The fish splashed, bucked, and bolted. I followed. Ian hollered. The line unzipped the river as the trout headed for deeper water—something they always do—and after about ten minutes I held a twenty-one-inch rainbow in my hands. A good Bow River fish, but because lots of trout between twenty-four and twenty-eight inches are caught each week during the summer, it wasn't one I'd be boasting about back at the shop. So I boasted to Ian instead. He promptly caught an identical rainbow, zipping my mouth shut.

All told, we hooked four big fish in the pool and landed three. Later, below a bend in the river known as the Cliffs of Doom, Ian landed a twenty-two-inch rainbow on a size 18 Elk Hair Caddis. In all, we probably caught half a dozen trout that day over twenty inches. I've spent three weeks in Montana, catching lots of fish, without getting *one* that size.

*   *   *

The red brick building where I work for the *Calgary Herald* sits high on an escarpment overlooking the city skyline and the Rocky Mountains. It's a great view, and I was lucky enough to grab a window seat when one became available. Out of the corner of that window, which runs the width of the newsroom, I can see the Bow River where it exits downtown and flows under a black trestle railway bridge. At least once a day I wander over to the window, place a foot on the ledge, and stare at the water. I imagine catching the trout that I know lurk right in the city. I daydream of playing hooky to get in a cast or two.

It's difficult to believe that cresting the rim of the lower Bow valley will bring the skyline of Calgary into view.

Once, during an especially frantic day at the office, I noticed something crawling on the window. I got up to look, and it was a pale morning dun, blown the half-mile from the river by a stiff southwesterly. There were other mayflies, too—a virtual hatch pressed against the window. I walked back to my desk and stared at the computer screen for awhile, but somehow the words just wouldn't come. I knew what those fish were doing down in the river, and it was almost too much to take.

No one comprehends cause and effect like a flyfisher. A bug on an office window can, reliably, portend rising fish a mile away. Give me a hot, windy afternoon in August, and I'll guarantee Bow River trout rising to grasshoppers ten miles away. Give me a rainy, blustery day in September, and I'll guarantee the same fish rising to blue-winged olives. In each case, it's simply a matter of following a sequence of natural events to a logical conclusion, a feat no different, really, than casting and knowing exactly where the fly will land.

American novelist Jim Harrison, after watching anglers get skunked on the Moscow River in the middle of the Russian capital and on the Seine in Paris, concluded that, "It is enough to have a river in a city." He should have visited Calgary.

Experienced Bow River flyfishers will tell you that if you want to catch a trophy brown trout—something in the thirty-inch range—the city's the place to be. Which may explain why it's not uncommon to see oil company executives swapping their suits and ties for chest waders during the corporate lunch hour—some of the highest office towers are only a double-haul away from the river.

Actually, having the quality of the fishing you'll find in the Bow in a city of 750,000 inhabitants is astounding. Equally amazing is the amount of water you'll have to yourself on any given summer evening. One of my favorite runs is a quarter-mile from the intersection of two freeways. Quite often I'll catch half a dozen brown trout between fifteen and twenty inches there on the way home from work. All the local flyrodders have a favorite spot in the city; trying to pry the secret from them is hopeless. Telling someone about a good pool at the end of a 4x4 rut a hundred miles from nowhere is one thing. Telling them about a good pool a block from your house is quite another.

Nonetheless, some of the popular spots do show up on the fishing maps. There's the Zoo Hole, Carburn Park, Mallard Point, the CIL Hole, and Poplar Island. Mike Day, a friend and Bow River guide, once told me a story about fishing the Zoo Hole well after dark. The hole is, of course, just below the zoo escarpment. As Mike blindly cast beneath a heavily-treed bank, he could hear the exotic birds screeching, the lions roaring. It was all very unnerving, he said, sort of like the scene in *Apocalypse Now* where the sailors develop a mango craving deep in the Cambodian jungle. Mike decided he'd had enough and turned to go. Whereupon he almost trampled a mallard hen and her ducklings.

"It scared me shitless," he said. "I almost fell backwards into the river."

Another guide, Dave Brown, recalled introducing John Gierach to the Bow in 1993. They floated through the heart of the city. At one point they drifted beneath a railway bridge where a worker was sandblasting concrete. Grit showered the boat. With characteristic wit, Gierach said, "I think I can honestly say that's the first time I've ever been sandblasted while fishing."

Ironically, the city itself has a lot to do with the great fishing. When Calgarians flush their toilets, they are inadvertently feeding the trout. It's yet another example of cause-and-effect. The city's sewage treatment plants dump phosphate and other nutrients into the river, and the nutrients promote weed growth. The weed beds provide shelter for the fish and aquatic insects. Trout eat the insects.

But it's a fine balance. Too much phosphate and the heavy weed growth starves the water of oxygen. Too little and the river is no more productive than an average stream. It's a balance that's constantly tipping one way or the other from year to year; fortunately, so far there hasn't been a major fish kill.

Population estimates range from about 1,500 to 2,500 catchable fish per mile, depending on the section and time of year (breeding rainbows leave the river in the spring to spawn, as do some browns in the fall). And while other western rivers such as the Bighorn and Missouri may have more fish, the growth rate of Bow River trout is phenomenal. A four-year-old fish is about nineteen inches long. Generally, brown trout predominate in the city, with the number of rainbows increasing as you travel downstream toward Carseland.

*   *   *

Predictably, a lot of novice Calgary flyrodders seem to take the Bow for granted. They fish it, catch a bunch of twenty-inch trout, and mutter "now what?" as if they've paid their dues and better things are in store. When you try to convince them that better things are *not* in store, that the Bow is just about as good as it gets, they roll their eyes, giving you a "Yeah, sure, whatever you say" sort of look. I should know; my wife's that way.

Christine has been flyfishing for a couple of years now, but she usually gets out on her terms, which basically means when the sun is shining and the nearest bear is fifty miles away. That's okay. I'd still rather spend a day fishing with her than just about anybody else, which probably explains why we're married.

Before our wedding Christine and I had a discussion about where to register and what we really needed in the way of gifts. Christine wanted dishes; I wanted fly rods. She wanted to register at a yuppie boutique; I wanted to register at a local fly shop.

"You *can't* register at a fly shop," she said.

"Why not?"

"Because I think it's ridiculous."

That sealed it; I resigned myself to plates and bowls. Thankfully, wedding guest Brian Anderson, a Bow River guide, gave us a one-day float trip instead.

As it turned out, more than a year passed before we managed to do the float. Still, we couldn't have picked a better day. It was late September and Indian summer—crisp, golden, and vivid. The clear fall air has a way of magnifying the Rockies on a day like that—it pulls the distant mountains closer, peeling away the miles. That's what I was thinking as we drove along Highway 24 to Carseland, past rolled straw bales, abandoned sheds, rusting farm equipment, dilapidated trucks, and all the other effluvia of prairie settlement. Brian had given us our choice of several floats; we opted for the one below the Carseland weir. This is a unique spot primarily because of its inaccessibility. A few miles below the weir, the Bow flows through an Indian reserve. At the time of this writing, their land is off-limits to non-native anglers. However, because the river itself is a public jurisdiction up to the high water mark—as are all of Alberta's rivers and creeks—the Indians can't stop you from floating there.

It so happens that Brian works for an outfitter that has access to a private put-in a few miles above the reserve. And although his float trips routinely venture into the reserve, the boat he uses has an outboard jet engine, so at the end of the day he simply motors back upstream. (Actually, "simply" might be stretching things a bit. He usually makes the return trip in near-darkness, and you quickly realize that your life is literally in Brian's hand on the outboard throttle.)

At the outset of our trip we agreed that Brian would spend time with Christine while I wandered off to do my own thing. Well, I hadn't wandered more than fifty yards from the first good pool they stopped to fish when I

Guide Brian Anderson with Christine Clarke and twenty-two inch lower Bow River rainbow.

heard Christine yelling. Seems Brian had hooked a big rainbow while show-ing her how to nymph properly, and by then he'd handed her the five-weight Thomas & Thomas, which was throbbing as the fish headed downstream in a fast tongue of current.

"How much backing on this thing?" Brian asked, eying the reel.

"At least 150 yards," I replied.

"Then I'd say you've got about ten yards left."

I scrambled for the boat, and we hopped in while Christine pressured the fish into stopping. When we'd caught up with it again, she jumped ashore to continue the fight. Now, at 115 pounds, Christine isn't a giant among fly-fishers. Fact is, she's a sprite. And after fifteen minutes or so of doing battle with that trout, the rod tip sagged badly and so did her spirits.

"I don't know if I can do this," she said, rotating her body sideways and tightening her arm against her body to gain leverage. "My arm's going numb."

"Here," I said, reaching for the rod. "I'll land him for you."

Wrong move. She gave me a look that stopped me cold.

"No way. This is between me and the fish." Eventually, the fish succumbed, and Brian succeeded in slipping a net under it. It was twenty-two inches of chrome-colored fish, a size 8 San Juan Worm lodged in its jaw. That fish set the tone for the rest of the day, which is to say, Christine caught big rainbows while I took pictures of them. One measured almost twenty-four inches.

"I can't figure this out," I said, as we floated through a particularly promis-ing stretch of submerged boulders and undulating green weeds. "Christine's nailing big fish, and all I'm getting is the odd twelve-incher."

"Oh," Christine interjected from the front of the boat, "so you're *count-ing* those."

Ouch!

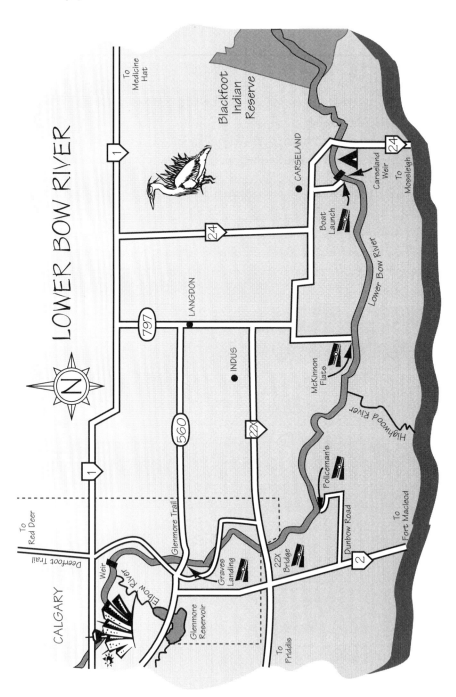

When You Go

Getting There

If you can find your way to Calgary, then you can find your way to the lower Bow River. As I mentioned, it flows through the city, and each year some of the biggest brown trout are caught within the city limits. With the fourth largest airport in Canada, Calgary is a major transportation hub. If you're driving up from Montana there are two routes to consider. Take Montana Highway 89 north of Browning and the Blackfeet Indian Reservation to the Canadian border and follow Highway 2 about 160 miles straight to Calgary. If you're driving up from Great Falls, Montana, follow Interstate 15 north to the border at Coutts and continue north on Highway 4 to Lethbridge. From there follow the signs to Highway 2 and Calgary, a distance of about 135 miles.

River Access

In Calgary there are dozens of bridges and other access points, including boat launches at Cushing Bridge, Bonnybrook, Graves Landing, and Highway 22X. (It's possible to do a great half- to full-day float trip without leaving the city, but expect the usual metropolitan quota of traffic noise and sirens.) If walking's your thing, pedestrian walkways parallel many of the prime stretches. Southeast of the city limits downstream to the Carseland weir (about fifty miles), much of the farmland overlooking the river valley is private and posted. Nevertheless, there are still at least half a dozen public access points and four convenient boat launches, so finding a place to fish is straightforward.

The most popular full-day floats for do-it-yourselfers are the Highway 22X bridge to McKinnon Flats and McKinnon Flats to the take-out just above the weir (one you don't want to miss!). Either float gives you all the fishing variety you could ask for. Still, I'd suggest hiring a good local guide for a day or two if you have the money and time. At the very least, you should pick up a detailed Bow River map from one of the shops mentioned below.

Equipment

Because the Bow is a big western river where wind can be a problem, leave your fancy one- and two-weight rods at home. Even for the most delicate dry-fly fishing, I never go lighter than a four-weight. Besides, only a masochist or a fool would attempt to play a twenty-five-inch rainbow on a three-weight rod. You might land the trout, but what kind of shape will you and the trout be in by the time you release it? My rod preferences for the Bow are as follows: a nine-foot, four- or five-weight for dries (six-weight if the wind's up); a fast five- or six-weight of the same length for nymphing; and a nine- to ten-foot, six-weight for throwing streamers.

Chest waders are a must on all but the hottest summer days, when you might be more comfortable wading wet. I prefer a heavy nylon wader (it's not as likely to puncture when jammed against beaver-gnawed branches), but the Bow runs cold all year and most local anglers choose neoprene. The Bow can also get slick as weed growth builds over the summer, so bring along felt-soled wading boots. Tippet material should range from 1X (streamers) to 5X (dry flies). Again, I've rarely had to go smaller than 5X on the Bow, and hooking a twenty-five-inch rainbow on 7X would be like lassoing a mustang with string.

As for clothing, pack for spring, summer, and fall every day of the season in Calgary (and the rest of Alberta, for that matter). Snow has fallen in all twelve months. And while things aren't usually that extreme, the weather can quickly change. A favorite Calgary expression is: "If you don't like the weather, just wait an hour." After all, those *are* mountains on the western horizon, so pack accordingly. Bring rain gear, sunscreen, and insect repellent. Come prepared for anything.

Fly Patterns

First, a tip. Whenever fishing in unfamiliar territory, one of the first things I do is drop by a fly shop and check which patterns they're sold out of—a dead giveaway to what's working. What works on the Bow are the usual assortment of western dries, nymphs, and streamers. For dries you'll want some Elk Hair and Goddard Caddis in sizes 10 to 18, Adams, Compara-duns, and PMD imitations in sizes 14 to 20, and an assortment of Trico Spinner and midge patterns in sizes 16 to 22. When the grasshopper season gets underway in August, you're going to want some Letort Hoppers and Stimulators in sizes 6 to 12; orange and yellow bodies work best.

Nymphs and emergers should include the usual smattering of Pheasant Tail, Gold-ribbed Hare's Ear, and Prince nymphs in sizes 12 to 18. Adding beadheads and flashbacks makes them even more effective. And don't forget some San Juan Worms, Bitch Creeks, and Girdle Bugs in sizes 6 to 10. The Worm, in particular, probably takes more Bow River trout each season than any other pattern.

For streamers, bring along Woolly Buggers, Clouser Minnows, and Bow River Buggers (a local pattern combining the body and marabou tail of a Woolly Bugger with the clipped deer-hair head of a sculpin imitation) in sizes 2 to 8. Popular colors are purple, brown, green, and black. That should do it. As guide Brian Anderson says, if you can't catch Bow River trout with those patterns, then the problem has nothing to do with your fly boxes.

Seasons and Tactics

Nymphing is the most productive method for early-spring fishing on the Bow. The San Juan Worm works well at this time of the year, as do attractor-style nymphs such as the Prince. Use lots of weight to get the flies down deep, because that's where most of the fish will be holding until they move into their summer lies. It's quite common to see midges hatching while the snow's still along the banks, but for some reason it usually takes the trout a while to warm up to them.

The first blue-winged olives start appearing about the middle of April; the first March browns at the beginning of May. (Obviously, whoever named this regal mayfly lived in a warmer climate than I do.) The March browns only come off for a couple of weeks, but when you hit this hatch right, it can be spectacular. Watch for overcast afternoons and have plenty of size 14 Dark Cahills on hand.

As far as I'm concerned, the Bow really comes into its own just after spring run-off, usually by the first week in July. I've already described the great streamer fishing to be had then; ditto for the midday PMD hatch. These pale yellow harbingers of summer start getting eaten as soon as the water clears enough for the trout to see them. The PMDs hatch daily until the end of the month, but just as their numbers start diminishing, the caddisfly hatches increase in intensity. Late July and August are the months to fish the Bow in the evening and into the night, when the caddisflies come off in staggering numbers. Start with a dry fly, but if that doesn't work, quickly switch to a LaFontaine Pupa or another emerger. Bow River trout are particularly choosy during this hatch, and once again, being adaptable is the key to success.

As the summer progresses, the early-morning Trico spinner fall attracts fly-rodders' attentions. I've found this to be a hit-and-miss proposition—sometimes the trout gulp mouthfuls of the tiny spinners, sometimes they ignore them altogether. More reliable, especially on windy, hot afternoons, is the grasshopper fishing. Concentrate on grassy banks where the naturals are blowing onto the water. Another good spot is at the base of sandstone bluffs and cliffs. The hopper fishing is good well into September, but by that time the blue-winged olives are hatching again, particularly on blustery days when you might be tempted to back out. Don't.

My thoughts have usually turned to bird hunting by October—to pheasant tails of a different sort—but this is a good time to get the Worms out again, and the autumn scenery can't be beat. The cottonwood and poplar leaves are a burnished gold, the sky so ceramic blue that it threatens to shatter and rain down upon the unsuspecting valley. This is also a good time to cast streamers. Use a sinking or sink-tip line and strip weighted Woolly Buggers through deep holes, where the trout are once again congregating as winter approaches.

Special Regulations

There are a number of special regulations on this section of the Bow (most within the city and pertaining to seasonal closures), so carefully read the *Alberta Guide to Sportfishing* included with your license. Highway 22X to the Carseland weir is open all year, and anglers are allowed to keep two trout under sixteen inches from June 1 to March 31. Personally, I practice catch-and-release ninety-nine percent of the time, and though I do occasionally kill a small trout or two for the frying pan, you couldn't pay me to eat a trout from the lower Bow (remember the treated sewage).

Places to Stay and Eat

There are dozens of hotels, motels, and private and provincial campgrounds in and around Calgary. The same goes for good restaurants. Your best bet is to contact the Calgary Convention & Visitors Bureau (237 8th Ave. S.E., Calgary, Alta., Canada, T2G 0K8; 800-661-1678 or 403-263-8510 in-province). The bureau can also arrange for guided trips.

Alberta Economic Development and Tourism (Commerce Place Building, 10155 102nd St., Edmonton, Alta., Canada, T5J 4L6; 800-272-9675 or 403-427-4321 in-province) publishes several useful travel planners and vacation guides. They include full listings of provincial campgrounds and other accommodations. Write for the current editions and a provincial highway map and you'll be able to plan a fishing excursion anywhere in Alberta.

Guides and Outfitters

Brian Anderson (403-249-8978) is a friend, a great guy, the person who taught me how to flyfish, and one of the Bow's best guides. Another good guy and great guide is Dave Brown (403-285-1668). Mike Day is a super guide and co-owner of Calgary fly shop Bow River Troutfitters (2122 Crowchild Trail N.W., Calgary, Alta., Canada, T2M 3Y7; 403-282-8868; bowriver@flyshop.com). Calgary's oldest fly shop, Country Pleasures (#570 Willow Park Village, 10816 Macleod Trail S., Calgary, Alta., Canada, T2J 5N8; 403-271-1016; bowriv@msn.com), can also put you in touch with reputable guides.

Other Attractions

With a population of about 750,000, Calgary has no shortage of things to do once the rods are put away. There's a great zoo and replica dinosaur park, Canada Olympic Park (site of the 1988 Winter Games), the Glenbow Museum, filled with native artifacts, and too many other attractions to mention here. If you're planning to come during the first two weeks of July, bring your cowboy boots and Stetson—that's when the world-famous Calgary Exhibition & Stampede transforms the city into a wild-west whoop-up.

2
Upper Bow River

One of my favorite reaches on the upper Bow River, that part of the river west of Seebe, flows past a lime plant. The plant is colossal and metallic and sends plumes of white smog drifting over the evergreens and down the valley. I know people work at the plant because I've seen their tiny outlines shuffling along the catwalks high in the air, but I've never met anyone there face-to-face. The plant is always operating, day and night, and getting used to its hum is part of the experience of fishing there.

One of the best holes along the reach is at a bend in the river near the "Hydrated Lime Test Section," where a dusting of lime coats the gravel along a railway track where hopper cars are loaded. I'd be tempted to call the bend the "Hydrated Lime Test Section Hole," but if I told people about it, they'd probably think I was fishing for bass or something.

I flyfish there for brown trout. They don't seem to mind the plant and its hum. Brown trout are like that—hardy and adaptable. The biggest brown I've caught in the upper Bow materialized at the tail of that bend one evening just before dusk. I could tell it was a big fish by the small puckers it left as it fed on the surface. I dropped a size 16 Elk Hair Caddis in its feeding lane and hung on when the hooked trout made for a driftwood branch lodged in the river. Somehow I managed to keep the fish clear of the tangle, and when I slipped a hand under the hen brown's yellowish belly, her lips came within half a foot of the first ferrule on the four-piece rod. Later I held a ruler against the graphite and measured twenty-two inches.

There are lots of smaller brown trout in the hole as well. During a hatch of sulphurs, the browns drift out from beneath the undercut bank and feed in pods, the larger fish always taking the prime spots. These trout often have the darker speckling and silvery flanks of sea-run or lake-strain browns. I've been told it has to do with the turquoise color of the upper Bow's glacier-fed water. Browns, more than any other trout, have a chameleon-like ability to blend in with their surroundings. A hundred miles downstream, east of Calgary, the lower Bow contains brown trout that more than live up to their name, ranging in color from taupe to burnished gold. To hold a brown from the lower Bow next to its upper-river counterpart, you'd swear they were different species.

The irony is that all Bow River brown trout—upper and lower—can trace their ancestry to an accidental stocking in 1925. It was then that a truck carrying 45,000 brown trout fry had an accident at the Carrot Creek Bridge upstream of Canmore. Realizing that his cargo would die before they could be stocked elsewhere, the driver released the fry into the Bow River tributary. Actually, the genetically-identical browns are one of the few things the upper Bow has in common with the lower river. Whereas the Bow east of Calgary flows through a wide cottonwood valley rimmed by prairie and grain fields, the upper Bow drains mountainous country replete with dense coniferous forests and boggy alpine meadows.

John Samms, a Canmore guide who specializes in the upper Bow and its environs, said there's no question the region's drawing card is its scenery. As strange as that might sound to someone staring at the lime plant or the excavated south face of Mount Exshaw, a major quarry, the fact is that upstream

With darker speckling and silvery sides, upper Bow River browns look like a different species than browns from the lower river.

of Dead Man's Flats the Bow River valley is indeed a spectacular setting. Anytime I fish there, I spend as much time looking up as I do down. The sky is pierced by mountains with names like Rundle and Cascade and Castle; the Three Sisters, a towering massif south of Canmore, look like three limestone molars set in a shale gum.

*   *   *

The Bow River rises as a tiny mountain stream at the foot of Bow Glacier in Banff National Park, 7,000 feet up in the main range of the Alberta Rockies. The glacier is actually an arm-like extension of a massive string of icefields stretching for several hundred miles along the continental divide. The Bow River headwaters are largely sterile—a result of elevation, extremely cold water, and a high concentration of glacial till and other sediment in the stream. Persevering flyrodders may catch a few small cutthroat, brook, or bull trout, but you're better off skipping the section of the river between Bow Lake and the junction of Highways 1 and 93 north of Lake Louise.

Downstream of Lake Louise the fishing quality improves considerably. The Bow is a typical mountain river there, with miles of pockets, plunge pools, tail-outs, and brushy banks. Most trout caught will be cutthroats averaging ten inches to a foot, but I've taken lots of fifteen-inch fish between Lake Louise and Banff. Rainbow trout increase in number as you approach Banff and Bow Falls; downstream of the falls, brown trout dominate.

Predictably, lots of anglers assume the fishing must be better in the national park, which begins west of Canmore and has clearly-marked boundary signs along the river. Not so. As Samms pointed out, the park is a "recovering fishery," abused and overfished for decades before the federal government got wise several years ago and toughened up the regulations. That said, the most productive flyfishing by far starts downstream of Canmore, where the river divides into a multitude of braids and channels, backwaters and lagoons. The preponderance of holding water will leave a neophyte flyfisher shaking his head, wondering where to begin, and the water is warm enough there to sustain good insect populations.

"We have a truly wild fishery here in the sense that the environment you're fishing in is *tough*," Samms said. Actually, "tough" might be an understatement. The upper Bow between Canmore and the lime plant can be as humbling as an overdrawn bank account.

"It's good, technically-challenging fishing," Samms added. When a guide says something like that, you know what he's really thinking is, "Jeez, I hope I don't get another rube in the boat today."

* * *

It was late July, and the upper Bow was just starting to clear after a prolonged run-off. The drive west from Calgary along Highway 1 is a geologic panorama, the blacktop gradually climbing from the prairies to the foothills to the mountains. As I drove past Dead Man's Flats, I thought of the French immigrant farmer killed there at the turn of the century by his ax-wielding brother. The brother was tried, found insane, and shipped off to an asylum.

I parked just west of Dead Man's Flats at a roadside pull-off. After rigging up, I had walked twenty yards into the spruce forest when a ruffed grouse exploded from behind a downed tree, its rapid wing beats jolting my heart into a similar cadence. When my pulse returned to normal, I heard a high-pitched whistle overhead. Glancing up, I spotted an osprey flying along the river, easily identifiable by its white underparts and the dark leading edges of its angled wings. It's always amazed me that a bird of prey could have such a timid squawk.

I reached the edge of the channel I'd come to fish, poking my head through a thicket of prickly wild rose to inspect the water. Dozens of little green stoneflies fluttered over the surface. It was late afternoon; I knew there'd be swarms of female stoneflies laying their eggs by evening. I heard a fish rise behind me along the bank and swung around in time to see the disturbed water coil downstream. A moment later the trout rose again. It was only a couple of feet from the bank, holding along the current seam behind a partially-submerged tree. I marked the spot where the trout was rising and slowly walked downstream until I was sure I wouldn't spook the fish. The channel was too deep to wade—the bank too tangled to make a proper cast from—so I crept up behind the trout until I could see it finning in the water. It was a brown of about sixteen inches.

What followed constituted a cast only in the technical sense. From a kneeling position, I grasped the size 14 Lime Trude between my left thumb and forefinger, pulled until the tip of the rod doubled back, and released the fly. It's called a bow-and-arrow cast, and its effectiveness in close quarters is an eye-opener.

The trout took the fly. Anticipating the brown's first move would be to swim into the submerged tree branches, I immediately jumped up and applied pressure to force it downstream. The ruse worked; about five minutes later I held the trout in the current to revive it, the fish's gill covers pumping hard to take in life-giving oxygen. I continued catching fish up and down the channel well into the evening, when the egg-laying stoneflies hung above the water like a vaporous hammock strung between the conifers.

* * *

If there's a serious threat to the upper Bow fishery, it's the rapacious hunger of short-sighted developers. For the most part, Banff National Park is off-limits. But in a contemporary re-enactment of the medieval siege, developers shunned by the park are doing everything they can to alter the landscape outside its east boundary. Environmentalists are doing their best to protect the so-called Canmore corridor, but unfortunately, for every resident who opposes the golf resorts and RV parks, there's someone else out to make a quick buck at nature's expense. Compounding matters is the fact that many

The Bow is a typical mountain river below Lake Louise, with miles of pockets, plunge pools, tail-outs, and brushy banks.

of the developers are either friends of politicians or ex-politicians themselves. Golf and politics have always been bedfellows, but the incestuous nature of the relationship is nevertheless appalling.

Fortunately, not all of the development along the corridor is repulsive. When the Stoney Indians built a lodge and convention facility at Hector Lake, they decided to retain the wetland rather than drain it and seed fairways in its place. The result is what's arguably the best stillwater rainbow trout fishery in Alberta. On any given summer weekend, dozens of float tubers and kick boaters descend on Hector to catch rainbows of up to twelve pounds. The lake is a lot like some of those on Montana's Blackfeet Reservation, which attracts stillwater anglers from throughout the world. The flyfishing is strictly catch-and-release at Hector (though reserve natives are still allowed to harvest fish), and there's a daily fee of about $15 (American).

Not up to Hector's caliber but still worth trying is Gap Lake, west of Exshaw along Highway 1A. It harbors brown trout to ten pounds, though they're extremely wary and hard to catch. I've had the best luck there just before dark on blustery evenings. Gap Lake also holds brook trout and mountain whitefish.

*   *   *

When I flyfish in the Canmore corridor, I often fish Hector Lake in the morning and early afternoon and then stash the kick boat and head over to the lime plant to fish the upper Bow until dark. It makes for a long but varied day, with a good chance of hooking big rainbows and browns in the same outing.

Just downstream of the bend below the lime plant, the channel widens, slows, and forms what is essentially a huge backwater. This glassy expanse, maybe the size of a football field and rarely more than a few feet deep, is locally known as the Mud Flats. During a good hatch of green drakes or pale morning duns or blue-winged olives, the brown trout leave the deeper lies and pools of the main river and congregate in pods to feed there.

"It's just like fishing a mud flat in a mangrove or tropical area," Samms noted. Earlier I described catching a twenty-two-inch upper Bow River brown, my personal best. Regrettably, I can only guess at the size of the fish I hooked and lost one evening on the Mud Flats. It took an Elk Hair Caddis, and following an agonizingly long moment in which the trout seemed to ponder its next stratagem, the fish tore across the flat toward the main channel and the

The upper Bow River is a truly wild fishery with browns, rainbows, brook trout, bull trout, cutthroats, and mountain whitefish.

faster current. And it never slowed down. Not at all. It just kept on going and going until the orange fly line on my six-weight spool was gone, headed down the river, and then until about fifty yards remained of the white backing attached to the fly line. At that point, I pointed my rod in the direction of the fish, some 150 yards distant, and squeezed the backing against the cork grip until the leader snapped. And that was that.

As a flyfisher, I spend an awful lot of time staring at water, wondering. I'm not sure what to make of this preoccupation with puddles—perhaps my karmic destiny is to be reincarnated as a fish. I do know that every time I drive past the lime plant on Highway 1—even if it's January and I'm on the way to Banff to ski—I stare over at the Mud Flats and think about that trout. I wonder if it's still there, and I wonder if I might catch it next spring.

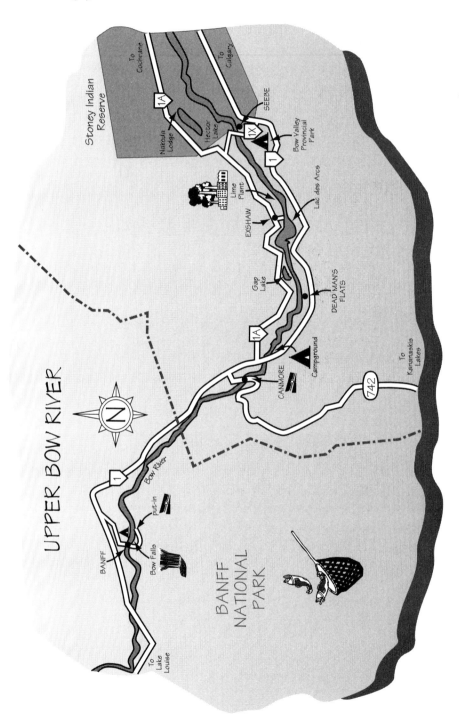

UPPER BOW RIVER

Stoney Indian Reserve

To Cochrane

To Calgary

1A

Natodia Lodge

Hector Lake

SEEBE

1X

Bow Valley Provincial Park

1

Lime Plant

EXSHAW

Lac des Arcs

Gap Lake

DEAD MAN'S FLATS

1A

Campground

CANMORE

To Kananaskis Lakes

742

N

Bow River

put-in

BANFF

Bow Falls

BANFF NATIONAL PARK

To Lake Louise

1

When You Go

Getting There

The best fishing on the upper Bow River is about an hour's drive west of Calgary on Highway 1. The highway parallels the river valley for many miles through the foothills and into Banff National Park.

River Access

There are numerous spots along Highway 1 to access the river, including Dead Man's Flats, the provincial campground east of Canmore, the Highway 1 bridge, and at Canmore itself. Inside the national park, access is unlimited. There are dozens of pull-offs along Highway 1 between Banff and Lake Louise, but keep in mind that this stretch receives lots of angling pressure throughout the summer.

Another option is to take the Seebe turn-off at Highway 1X and drive north to Highway 1A. Also known as the Bow Valley Parkway, this two-lane blacktop provides good access to the river between Seebe and Canmore. Much of the land is private, but the property owners are generally cooperative, and there are at least a half-dozen public access points at towns and day-use sites.

For those planning do-it-yourself float trips on the upper Bow, there's really only one stretch I can recommend—the put-in is just downstream of Bow Falls at the Banff townsite, and the take-out is under the main Canmore bridge. This is a relatively straightforward full-day float, but you'll need to keep an eye out for log jams and sweepers, particularly downstream of the clearly-marked national park boundary. Also note that because the float begins in Banff National Park, you'll need a park day pass and fishing license in addition to the standard Alberta angling license. (See the "Special Regulations" heading for more details.)

Resist any temptation to float the river between Canmore and Seebe. This infamous stretch of braided channels, river-blocking log jams, and dead-end backwaters has destroyed enough boats to earn the nickname "canoe eater." I prefer to walk-and-wade this section anyway, but if you're intent on floating it, contact one of the guides listed below and book a trip with him.

Equipment

The best all-round rod for the upper river is probably an eight-and-a-half- or nine-foot, five-weight. That said, I usually find myself using a six-weight if I'm fishing from a boat or casting along the main channel or a four-weight if I'm concentrating on the braids, backwaters, lagoons, and beaver ponds. (Because the latter sort of fishing is often in heavy brush with limited casting space, I prefer a shorter rod in those situations, maybe an eight-foot.) The bankside willows and dense woods along the smaller braids and backwaters also offer protection from the wind, so casting the lighter rod is rarely a problem.

When selecting leaders and tippet material for the upper Bow, keep in mind the wary, cautious nature of the wild brown trout. I usually fish leaders of between twelve and fourteen feet, a habit I picked up while in New Zealand. You may not be comfortable with a leader that long but use the longest you can. Although a 3X tippet will work fine during a golden stonefly hatch in choppy water, I frequently go as light as 6X when casting small dry flies to large browns in slicks or backwater lagoons.

You'll want to wear chest waders, but while neoprene is fine for float trips or other open-water fishing, I don't venture into the woods along the upper Bow without reinforced nylon waders. Why? Because I'm tired of spending as much money on Aquaseal as I do on sunscreen—the wild rose thickets and beaver-sharpened saplings along the side channels take no prisoners. As usual, flyfishers should also bring along plenty of warm clothing, rain gear, and insect repellent.

Fly Patterns

Bring the same flies to the upper river that you would to the lower Bow downstream of Calgary. (See the "Fly Patterns" listing in that chapter.) However, you'll need several additional patterns for the upper Bow as well. Dark brown or black Elk Hair Caddis (sizes 10 to 18) are a good imitation of the little brown stoneflies that emerge throughout the winter and early spring. Yellow-bodied Grizzly Wulffs (sizes 10 to 16) will imitate the sulphur duns. A yellow-bodied Stimulator or Improved Sofa Pillow (sizes 8 to 14) is a good golden stonefly imitation, and when trout are rising to little yellow and little green stoneflies, try a Lime Trude (sizes 14 to 18).

Seasons and Tactics

Although portions of the upper Bow remain ice-free all winter, I don't recommend fishing there until the spring breakup in late March or early April. Walking along the frozen side-channels and backwaters is just too risky unless you really know the area and the water.

Anglers can usually count on a month or two of decent flyfishing prior to run-off, which generally begins by late May. Along the river's main channel, try fishing weighted nymphs through the deep pools, beside downed timber, and along undercut banks. Suggested patterns include the San Juan Worm, Beadhead Prince, Zug Bug, Montana, and Bitch Creek nymphs in sizes 6 to 14. Flyrodders should also watch for several species of aquatic insects that emerge at this time of the year. The little brown stoneflies tend to show up on warmer afternoons, but even when they're present in good numbers, the trout often ignore them. By mid-April, the first caddisflies start hatching. Typically, they're the so-called skittering caddis, and like the little brown stoneflies, the greatest concentrations usually appear during the afternoon along well-oxygenated riffles. If there are caddisfly adults on the water but the trout aren't taking them, try fishing a soft-hackle wet fly just beneath the surface to imitate the natural pupa. Caddisflies continue to be a staple for upper Bow River trout throughout the summer and into the fall.

Run-off often lasts into July, but fortunately, the upper Bow still affords flyfishers some unique angling opportunities at this time. Even when the river's main channels are muddy and unfishable, intrepid flyfishers willing to seek out the flooded backwaters, lagoons, and oxbows will often be rewarded with exceptional fishing.

"At no time up here are you shut out," noted Canmore guide John Samms. The reasoning is straightforward—the brown trout don't like the muddy water any more than you do, and as soon as the river starts clouding, they move into slower, clearer water and sheltered lies. Stalking the big browns in these flooded thickets requires patience and skill. As Samms pointed out, successful anglers will spend a lot more time *watching* than *casting*.

The end of run-off marks the beginning of the most consistent and fruitful dry-fly fishing on the upper Bow. The best angling is almost always on overcast days and in the evening.

"The river here does not fish well on a bright, sunny day," Samms conceded. The golden stoneflies, little green stoneflies, and yellow sallies (little yellow stoneflies) emerge as soon as the main channels clear. And because the upper Bow is a cold river at a higher elevation, these hatches and others usually continue much later in the summer than they do on other Alberta streams. During July and August, there are also good mayfly hatches of pale morning duns, green drakes, sulphurs, and blue-winged olives, the latter picking up in September. However, these hatches often overlap, and flyfishers should pay particular attention to which insect the trout are feeding on.

Finally, late September and early October usually bring sporadic but promising hatches of giant orange sedges. Also known as fall caddis, the huge adult naturals (sizes 6 to 10) are typically seen late in the evening as they dip onto the water to oviposit their eggs. I imitate them with a big orange-bodied Stimulator or Bucktail Caddis skittered across the surface.

Special Regulations

The upper Bow River can be fished all year with one exception: the stretch from the Highway 1 bridge near Canmore downstream to the mouth of Pigeon Creek (near Dead Man's Flats) is closed from October 1 to December 15 to protect spawning brown trout. However, the local chapter of Trout Unlimited is pushing to strengthen the regulations even further.

"We need some slot sizes, and we need bait prohibited," Samms said, pointing out that the number of brown trout killed by anglers each year on the upper Bow is preposterous.

As noted, anglers fishing in Banff National Park will also require a park pass and fishing license. The pass is about $4 (American) per person and $7.50 for a group; angling licenses are $4.50 per week or $10 per season.

Places to Stay and Eat

As international tourist destinations, both Canmore and Banff have plenty of accommodations to suit any traveling tastes—everything from campgrounds to five-star hotels. Likewise, there are dozens of top-notch restaurants and bars. Contact the Canmore-Kananaskis Chamber of Commerce (P.O. Box 1178, Canmore, Alta., Canada, T0L 0M0; 403-678-4094) or the Banff-Lake

Louise Tourism Bureau (P.O. Box 1298, Banff, Alta., Canada, T0L 0C0; 403-762-0270).

Guides and Outfitters

John Samms and the guides at Mountain Fly Fishers (P.O. Box 2414, Canmore, Alta., Canada, T0L 0M0; 403-678-2915) offer float trips, walk-and-wade fishing, backcountry fly-in fishing, and float tubing on area lakes and ponds. Another reputable outfitting service is Banff Fishing Unlimited (P.O. Box 216, Canmore, Alta., Canada, T0L 0M0; 403-762-4936 or through Wapiti Sports at 403-678-5550).

Other Attractions

The Bow River valley through the Canmore corridor and Banff National Park is filled with things to do and places to see. The mountainous hiking and backpacking is spectacular and will remind American visitors of the rugged wilderness at Glacier National Park in Montana or Colorado's Rocky Mountain National Park. Banff and area attractions worth visiting include the Buffalo Paddock, Lake Louise, Cave and Basin sulphur hot springs, historic Banff Springs Hotel and adjacent Bow Falls, the Banff Park Museum with its impressive wildlife collection, and the glacier-riddled Icefields Parkway north of Lake Louise. For more information, contact the Banff-Lake Louise Tourism Bureau (403-762-0270) or any of the park's tourist information centers.

3
Highwood River

For the most part, flyfishing isn't what I'd consider a high-risk activity. Slippery streambeds and fast currents have claimed a few victims over the years; sharp hooks have bloodied more than a few fingers and ears. And I saw a photograph once of a flyfisher with a tiny nymph embedded in his eye. The photo made me nauseous.

I guess I'm not what you'd consider a risk-taker, having outgrown the need to impress either myself or others. There is, however, one place I make an exception: the Highwood River "gorge." I love the gorge. I love its sinewy curves, its black bedrock outcroppings. I love its depth and its spatial extremes. I love the way light and shadow cleave the water and the air, the river a sundial with hundred-foot conifers casting shade that traces the sweep of the sun across the sky. By midsummer, the water's surface is as clear and polished as a corrective lens, enhancing the scarlet sides on the rainbow trout that waver beside pale limestone walls in aquamarine pools. The trouble is that access to the gorge is not without real danger.

The gorge begins just west of Longview and extends upstream for about twenty miles. Longview is a village of about 300 people. The oil pumpjacks, strewn across the countryside like erect crickets, denote the region's petroleum deposits. In 1936, nearby oil discoveries sparked a boom, and one of the towns that emerged was Little New York, so named because of its rapid growth and metropolitan flavor. Less than ten years later, another oil boom in central Alberta lured most of the inhabitants away; suddenly "Little New York" seemed a bit ostentatious, and the village was renamed Longview. The area's other mainstay industry is ranching, and some of Alberta's most famous spreads are situated in the Highwood River valley. The EP Ranch, southwest of Longview, was once owned by the Duke of Windsor.

Driving west on Secondary Highway 541, crossing streams with names like Sullivan, Flat, and Deep, it's easy to see how British royalty could have been smitten by the treed foothills and glaciated peaks. If I had the money, I'd probably buy a ranch along the Highwood as well, though these days it would take millions of dollars or the crown jewels. Fortunately, the ranchers that *do* live there are generally a good-natured lot; many encourage public access to the river through wooden stiles along the barbed-wire fences. Of course, walking through the Z-shaped stiles (cow-proof) could be the simplest ambulatory feat you perform all day. The real fun begins at the rim of the gorge, where choosing a route down to the water will test your mountaineering savvy and push the limits of the no-risk envelope. My descents usually include some combination of sliding, grabbing, and falling. A good idea is to keep a four-piece rod in its tube on the way down. An even better idea is to wear protective gloves and a climbing helmet.

* * *

To most southern Alberta flyrodders, the Highwood River is "that place the Bow River rainbows go to spawn." In fact, the Highwood watershed represents the only spawning habitat available to the lower Bow River's world-famous rainbow trout. Most of these fish have returned to the "big river" by the time the Highwood opens to angling in mid-June, but some inevitably lag or stay behind, creating quite an impression when a flyfisher hooks one of these outsized holdovers in the tight confines of the Highwood canyon. The water there is unrelenting—even more so when there's an eighteen-inch rainbow on the end of the line. If the trout decides to turn tail and run downstream, disappearing into the foamy whorl of plunge pools and staircase rapids, say goodbye.

This section also harbors cutthroat and bull trout. Farther upstream, in the Kananaskis Country forest reserve, there are occasional small brook trout, too. The upper Highwood begins at the junction of Storm and Mist creeks, names that, unfortunately, accurately reflect the bulk of the weather at the 6,000 foot elevation. (Some of the larch and fir trees in this area are more than 350 years old, attesting to the short growing season and harsh climate.) The river at that altitude isn't as fertile as it is east of the forest reserve, but a little exploration will usually yield a decent fish or two. Unlike the gorge, where the streambed consists predominantly of shale ribs running at right angles to the current (picture the traverse strips in the hull of a bark canoe), the upper Highwood has a freestone bottom. It's a beautiful, remote stretch of water, but I rarely fish there anymore, and when I do, I'm casting for nostalgia more than anything else.

That pretty much sums up how I feel about the lower Highwood as well, a section of the river as different from the upper reaches as a man's foot is from

The real fun begins at the rim of the Highwood River gorge, where choosing a route down tests your mountaineering savvy and pushes the limits of the no-risk envelope.

his head. East of High River, a prairie town along Highway 2, the Highwood meanders through what has basically become the southern fringe of Calgary's urban sprawl. It's one thing to be fishing the lower Highwood after dark and see the northern sky glowing from the city lights; it's quite another to be driving along a "country" road and come across a green sign for 546th Avenue. Predictably, public access to the lower Highwood is limited. Keep in mind that even if you access the river via a bridge or obliging landowner's property, Alberta law still dictates that you stay below the high-water mark. Nevertheless, if you can manage to ignore the BMWs, horizon-blocking houses, and satellite dishes, the river does have its merits.

Deep pools hug the contours of tan sandstone bluffs; garter snakes slip into the water as your footfalls startle them out of daytime idylls. Fishing upstream, I like to pause frequently along the shore, maybe searching out a boulder to sit on while I scan the water for rises. Sure enough, on those hot summer afternoons it isn't long before a grasshopper comes floating by, spinning round and round in the current like a crazed compass needle. The hoppers never last long below the bluffs, where vigilant rainbows gaze upwards and await the struggling terrestrials. I use a Letort Hopper with a vermilion-colored body. Don't be shy; cast so it splats on the water just upstream of where the trout last rose. If necessary, give the fly a twitch. Be patient. Trout will often cruise when feeding on hoppers, and it may take several casts before the fish notices the artificial.

Because of the relatively sedate water and abundance of weeds below Highway 2, the lower Highwood also has good summertime hatches of pale morning duns and several species of caddisflies. The rainbows are smallish (most between six and ten inches), but casting to them on the riffles and flats makes for great sport on a muggy August evening. One of my favorite pastimes is to try and distinguish between the rising trout and the rising whitefish. And I don't care what anyone says—hooking a foot-long whitefish on a small dry fly requires more skill than hooking a trout of comparable size. Whitefish have soft mouths and finicky dispositions; those flyrodders who boastfully hurl them into the bushes should be flogged.

On slow evenings I'm content to watch the schools of rainbow trout fry swimming in the backwaters, thin as pencil leads. Seeing them always makes me think of the Bow River, where the fry will travel when they're old enough to leave the nursery. I think it's ironic that the fry, which represent natural renewal in the truest sense, live in the shadow of satellite dishes. Mention "fish fry" to the resident acreage dwellers, and most of them will think of the office barbecue and not of the stream flowing past their backyards.

*   *   *

Just as the trout fry will swim downstream to the Bow River when nature ordains it, at some point each summer my own instincts lead me upstream to revisit the gorge. We all have our callings. The drive south from Calgary takes me past yellow canola fields and purple thistle, past silver grain silos and green aspens. The countryside is a shimmering spectrum, the wind rippling the colors so they run together like oils on an artist's palette.

Every flyfisher has a couple of days a season that are so tremendous, so fulfilling, that they bleed into memory and stain the consciousness. Sometimes they're the days when you catch a mess of trout; other times they're the days when you catch a cold beer tossed your way by a fishing companion, too exhausted to struggle out of your chest waders, too relaxed to care.

I had one of those memorable days a couple of years ago in the Highwood gorge. The sky was uniformly blue when I set out that morning. Even the

Ian Thomson fishes the Highwood River, "that place the Bow River rainbows go to spawn."

scattered cumulus clouds that marshal their forces over the mountains before drifting east had failed to materialize. I parked my Nissan 4x4, checked the contents of my day pack, and set out for one of my favorite sections of the river. Rather than struggle through the thigh-high grass in the quarter-mile of meadow leading to the canyon, I hugged a fence line—it's a good trick in cattle country, where nine times out of ten the cows will trample a path along a fence. Near the river I left the path and cut through a grove of aspens. White common yarrow and bluebells grew among clusters of yellow-flowered shrubby cinquefoil, which seems to bloom from ice-off to freeze-up.

At the edge of the gorge, I surveyed the defensive alignment and called an audible, abandoning my usual route for what appeared to be a scree seam between the rock coverage. However, the hole closed sooner than I'd anticipated, and halfway down I had to reverse my field, swinging from spruce boughs like Tarzan. I reached the end zone by jumping the last ten feet. Someday I'm sure a helicopter is going to have to pluck me from the gorge on a forty-foot rope, but until then I'll take my chances.

The river made the only noise, a dull rumble that reverberated off the shale crags. The sun barely cleared the south canyon wall, and I had my choice of fishing the dazzling water at my feet or the dark water along the far bank. I chose the former. The river danced and sparkled, whirled and sent flecks of foam spraying in the air. From beneath its transparent skin, I pulled fourteen-inch rainbows. Their backs were as emerald green as the pools they came from. They fought spectacularly, too, leaping and twisting, strengthened by the cold water and forceful current. The trout were larger at the heads of the pools; often I could see them rising through eight feet of water to hit my attractor dry flies—size 12 Lime Trudes and Royal Wulffs. Study the water if you like, but my fly selection in the gorge begins by glancing skyward. The columnar shafts of sunlight piercing the spruce trees silhouette any flying insects, and the golden stones and yellow sallies look like they've been hung in a display case.

By the end of the day I'd probably landed several dozen trout. One was seventeen inches, no doubt a Bow River holdover as captivated by the Highwood gorge as I. In time, perhaps, it will return to the big river. But I hope not. You see, I now know where that trout resides—I know exactly which undercut ledge it swam out from to take my fly. I'd like to think that rainbow will still be there when I return to the gorge next summer, but that might be a risky assumption.

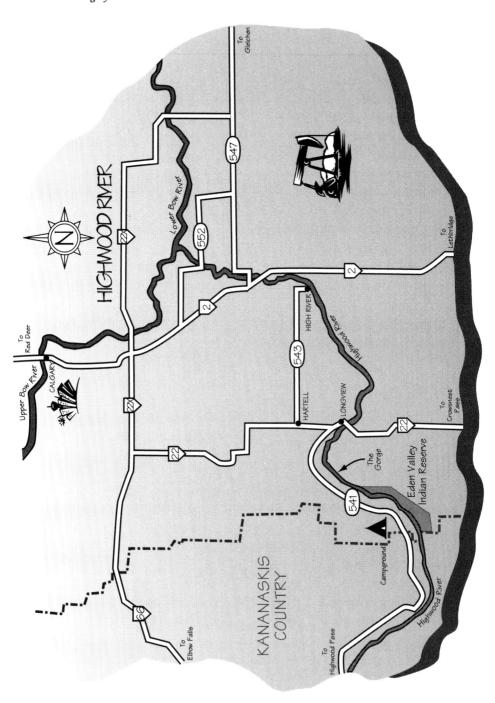

When You Go

Getting There

To reach Longview from Calgary, take Highway 22X west for eleven miles and then turn south on Highway 22 and continue for thirty miles. A highway bridge crosses the Highwood River just past the southern outskirts of town. To reach the Highwood gorge and, eventually, the Kananaskis Country forest reserve, turn west onto Secondary Highway 541 at the north end of Longview. The highway parallels the river valley for many miles, occasionally providing spectacular views of the Highwood gorge on the south side of the road. To reach High River from Calgary, drive thirty miles south on Highway 2. You can also get from High River to Longview by following Secondary Highway 543 west to Hartell and then taking Highway 22 south for five miles to Longview.

From Montana, follow Interstate 15 north to the border; then follow Highway 4 for seventy miles to the junction with Highway 3 at Lethbridge. Drive thirty-five miles west to the junction with Highway 2 and drive north for about sixty-five miles to High River.

River Access

Access is unlimited in the Kananaskis Country forest reserve west of Longview. Downstream of the reserve boundary, which includes the best fishing in the gorge, the river flows through private ranchland, and you'll have to seek permission. (Anglers should also be aware that the Eden Valley Indian Reserve is just east of the Kananaskis Country boundary, and fishing is confined to the Highwood's north bank.) Fortunately, several of the landowners along Secondary Highway 541 to Longview permit access through wooden stiles installed in the fence line. Some of these are close to the road, and you shouldn't have much trouble spotting them.

There's also access at the Highway 22 bridge at Longview, but below that public access is limited. The Highwood flows through mixed ranch- and farmland downstream to High River; you'll need permission to fish throughout this section. There's some public access at High River. East of the town the best bets are bridge crossings at Highway 2 and at Secondary Highways 552 and 547 upstream of the Highwood's confluence with the Bow River.

Equipment

In terms of equipment and fly patterns, it's probably easiest to divide the river into two sections: the upper Highwood (above Longview), and the lower Highwood (downstream of Longview to the confluence with the Bow River).

With its recurring sluice pools, tail-outs, and pocket water, the upper Highwood is perfectly suited to lighter rods—say, an eight-foot, four-weight—and stout tippets. I'll go as large as 3X on some of the rougher sections in the gorge, but 4X is the norm. Leader length isn't as important here as it is on the lower Highwood; I usually opt for seven-and-a-half or nine-foot lengths. The Highwood valley can be windy, but the gorge is well protected and the wind generally doesn't pose as much of a problem there as it does on some of the province's other trout streams. Besides, the rock outcroppings always provide some sort of shelter as you make your way along this section, and typical casts are less than thirty feet.

Unfortunately, the same can't be said for the lower Highwood, which often flows through exposed countryside. This is a good place to take a nine-foot, five-weight rod. The river also slows as it leaves the foothills; the slicks are more pronounced and the trout have more time to contemplate flies. Have some 5X and 6X tippet on hand and longer leaders.

More often than not, especially in the gorge, I wade wet. The steep climb is arduous enough without chest waders, and though the Highwood water is frigid, I'm rarely in the river much except to cross back and forth. I find that a pair of nylon wind pants takes the chill off cooler days. If the weather is really lousy or if it's early or late in the season, I take neoprene chest waders along just in case. Chest waders also come in handy on the lower river, where you'll probably be spending more time standing in the water, particularly during heavy hatches when the trout are rising over the width of the stream.

Bring along the usual Alberta compliment of clothes and accessories. One of the most miserable nights I ever spent in a tent was beside an alpine lake overlooking the Highwood River valley. When I set out with two friends that June weekend the temperature was in the seventies and the sky cloudless. Later that same day it was sleeting. When we parted the tent flaps the next morning, there was eight inches of snow. Foolishly, I'd left my down sleeping bag at home and brought along a cheap synthetic one instead. I shivered all night, and if not for the warm bodies on either side of me, it would have been worse.

Fly Patterns

On the upper section, I almost always start out with an attractor dry fly in the gorge, something like a size 8 to 14 Royal Wulff, Stimulator, or Letort Hopper. If the trout aren't taking the dry, tie an eighteen-inch section of leader to the bend in the hook and attach a small nymph; my favorites are the Beadhead Prince and Gold-ribbed Hare's Ear, sizes 12 to 18.

I rarely spend a day on this section without seeing at least a few trout rising to yellow sally stoneflies. The best imitation continues to be a small Lime Trude (sizes 14 to 18). Finally, no trip to the upper river would be complete without taking along a few drab "catch-all" patterns, such as Adams and Irresistibles in sizes 12 to 18.

Take the same assortment of patterns to the lower river, but be prepared for some good pale morning dun and caddisfly hatches as well. To imitate the naturals try Borger Yarn Wing Duns or Compara-duns (sizes 12 to 20) and Elk Hair or Goddard Caddis (sizes 10 to 18). It's also a good idea to bring along some big Gray Wulffs to imitate the brown drakes that hatch sporadically along the slower, silt-bottomed sections.

Seasons and Tactics

The Highwood and its tributaries don't open to angling until mid-June; by then run-off is usually in full swing and can last well into July. I try to make it to the upper river as soon as the water starts clearing, because the golden stones are usually still around and the rainbows eagerly accept big dry-fly imitations such as yellow-bodied Stimulators. This is also a good time of the year to try yellow sally patterns—an effective combination is a Lime Trude dry fly as an indicator with a small Gold-ribbed Hare's Ear nymph tied to a dropper. (I tie my nymphs with yellow dubbing.) Farther downstream, around High River, watch for heavy pale morning dun hatches from late June through July.

Flyfish the Highwood as you would any other freestone stream: the margins, heads, and tails of pools are always good bets. And take your time. Scrutinize the water carefully; the clarity often makes for good sight fishing (unusual in Alberta), so you might as well take advantage of it. Keep a low profile, and don't be reluctant to fish blind as well, especially in the gorge. You'll be surprised how often a trout will materialize from hidden structure to take a fly.

As the summer progresses, the grasshopper fishing picks up over the length of the river. Watch for naturals along the banks and don't hesitate to try a Letort Hopper; cast it to land with a *plop* to get the trout's attention. The best hopper fishing is below vertical cliffs rimmed by grassland (where you can always count on a few hoppers to take a wrong turn) and along grassy banks buffeted by wind.

As mentioned, the brown drakes hatch periodically during the summer along the lower Highwood. The evening caddisfly hatches on the same section can be profuse. Above all, don't leave the water too early in the evening—as is the case on the nearby Bow River, the best flyfishing is often after sunset. The caddisfly hatches continue into the fall, but by then reduced water levels and a stampede of whitefish-seeking bait anglers tend to dampen my enthusiasm.

Special Regulations

The Highwood River and its tributaries are open to flyfishing from June 16 to October 31. Check the regulations if you plan to keep any rainbow or cut-throat trout, but keep in mind that all trout under ten inches long must be released. (Because the Highwood and its tributaries are the only spawning habitat available to lower Bow River rainbows, I put back all the trout I catch.)

Places to Stay and Eat

Depending on which section of the river you intend to fish, the Highwood is anywhere from a thirty-minute to a two-hour's drive from Calgary. For information on hotels, motels, campgrounds, and restaurants, contact the Calgary Convention & Visitors Bureau (237 8th Ave. S.E., Calgary, Alta., Canada, T2G 0K8; 800-661-1678 or 403-263-8510 in-province).

High River also has plenty of accommodation and dining. Contact the town Chamber of Commerce (Box 5244 High River, Alta., Canada, T1V 1M4; 403-652-3336). There are a couple of motels and restaurants in Long-view, including the wonderful Memories Inn Restaurant. Proprietor Bernard "Rudy" Vallee serves tall tales and prime rib with equal aplomb. Clint Eastwood fell in love with the place while filming the Academy Award-winning west-ern *Unforgiven* in the nearby foothills. Eastwood's outhouse from the movie set adorns the yard next door, though Rudy insists it's for display only and still asks patrons to use the flush toilet. Not surprisingly, Memories Inn has become a big hit with Calgarians, and you'll need to reserve a table all summer long (403-558-3665).

If camping's your thing, there are several provincial and private campgrounds along Secondary Highway 541 west of Longview. Most of these are right on the Highwood River.

Guides and Outfitters

A few Calgary guides will take you flyfishing to the Highwood, but you'll have to specifically request a trip there. Tell them you want to fish the gorge west of Longview and leave it at that. Try Mike Day at Bow River Troutfitters (2122 Crowchild Trail N.W., Calgary, Alta., Canada, T2M 3Y7; 403-282-8868; bowriver@flyshop.com). Another guide who does trips west of Calgary is Brian Anderson (403-249-8978).

Other Attractions

The Kananaskis Country forest reserve west of Longview has some marvelous hiking trails, and the Highwood Pass near the river's headwaters is the highest paved road in Canada at almost 7,000 feet. About eight miles south of Longview, near the junction of Highway 22 and Secondary Highway 540, is the Bar U, a restored national historic site and representative foothills ranch. In High River, drop by the Museum of the Highwood, housed in the town's original sandstone train station. For Calgary, see the listings in Chapter 1 on the lower Bow River.

Part Two

South of Calgary

4
Crowsnest River

I always expect to see them hatching from eggs, clawing their way through broken shells, wet and gleaming. Like chicks, or dinosaurs. Even the name sounds prehistoric: *Pteronarcys*—the giant stoneflies. *Pteronarcys californica*, commonly known in Alberta as the salmonfly, is the biggest of them all—a lumbering beast that clatters in flight, its wings rattling like dishes on a shelf as a train passes by. Reaching up to three inches in length, the adults are dark brown or black on top and reddish-orange on the bottom. The color of the abdomen is reminiscent of sockeye flesh, hence the name salmonfly.

This is the bug that sets the Crowsnest River (known locally as the "Crow") apart from all other Alberta trout streams. For though the salmonfly lives elsewhere, nowhere else does it hatch as reliably or profusely. In fact, during a good year, the Crowsnest salmonfly hatch is every bit as celebrated as the famous emergences south of the border on rivers such as the Big Hole and Madison, which attract flyfishers from around the world.

Sometime about mid-May, when the first wild violets begin flowering along the Crow's banks, two- to four-year-old salmonfly nymphs start migrating toward shore, where they crawl onto rocks or streamside foliage. It's there that the adults emerge, usually at night or in the early morning. During a heavy emergence, the adults cover the willow and aspen branches, the leaves and the grasses. I've seen small bushes so overloaded with salmonflies that they sag, like a Christmas tree with too many ornaments.

The adults mate and the females then return to the water to lay their eggs. This is a fascinating event, both from a fishing and an entomological point of view. Sometimes the females will actually brush the water's surface in flight, using tension to pry the eggs loose. Other times the females never do touch the water, dropping the egg clusters payload-style from varying altitudes. The trout, meanwhile—often some of the biggest fish in the river—are roused to near-madness, slashing at the awkward salmonflies with bacchanalian abandon. Most of the time.

This so-called "brush hatch," as Alberta angling writer Bob Scammell calls it, doesn't always unfold as planned. Unfortunately, by the time the hatch is in full swing, say by late May or early June, the Crow is occasionally running high and muddy from mountain run-off. The trout, of course, can't see a darned thing, and after driving two-and-a-half hours south of Calgary at reckless speeds, you resign yourself to pool tables and an afternoon at the pub.

Not to worry. Following years of driving at reckless speeds and sinking too many eight balls, I'd like to pass along the following advice: anglers that bank everything on the dry-fly fishing should reconsider their tactics and restock their fly boxes. Remember those migrating nymphs, the ones headed for shore back in mid-May when the water was low and clear? The trout eat them by the thousands. Even once the "brush hatch" is underway, you'll catch a lot more fish by drifting a size 6 Montana or Bitch Creek nymph along the bottom than you will by fishing dries on top.

The most productive day I've had on the Crow took place a couple of years ago during the last week in May, when friend Kevin Watson and I stopped there for a few days on the way home from a Montana trip. Parking the camper, we

What sets the Crowsnest River apart from other Alberta rivers is the salmonfly hatch, which brings up the biggest fish.

decided to tackle the stretch between the Burmis Lake and Highway 507 bridges. The flyfishing around Burmis is excellent. Rainbows in the fourteen-to eighteen-inch range predominate, and occasionally you'll hook one a lot bigger. Toss in a few cutthroats, the odd brookie, and the ubiquitous mountain whitefish, and the menu is complete. The scenery isn't anything to scoff at, either. With the Flathead mountain range as a backdrop, the Crowsnest is the one constant in an ever-changing landscape, the river valley descending from slab rock to fur-treed foothills to aspen groves to grass pasture. All that in the course of a day's walk, which is exactly what Kev and I had in mind.

Sheets of gray clouds hung suspended between the foothills; the woods were perfectly still, damp and pungent in the uniform light. Even the rain couldn't decide whether to fall or not, starting and stopping, starting and stopping, making us don jackets one moment and doff them just as quickly. A day like that is timeless, the sun irrelevant. Ten o'clock, noon, two o'clock … who knows? Who cares?

"What are you tying on?" Kev asked.

"A Montana Nymph—maybe a Worm on the dropper. Lots of weight. You?"

"A Worm—maybe a Prince Nymph."

We split up. We caught fish. Lots of them. Rarely more than fifty feet across, the Crow is the sort of river tailor-made for walk-and-wade flyfishers. To try and navigate it in a boat would be to take your life in your hands. If a sweeper or midstream boulder didn't get you, an outraged angler would. Every so often Kev and I met as we leapfrogged our way up the river, our eyes glazed, our hands shaking. Words tumbled out like water over a cataract.

"Unbelievable!"

"Twenty-three inches!"

"Fantastic!"

I recall standing on a gravel shore where the current swept around a bend, casting my double-nymph rig into the throat of a mysterious blue pool on the inside corner. Tiny white bubbles rose to the surface in the turbulent wash. Time and again big rainbows jerked the orange indicator beneath the surface, usually taking the stonefly imitation, sometimes the Worm. I caught half a dozen trout, only moving my feet when I had to follow one downstream. My hands got cold; my resolve numb. Finally I just walked away, not because I'd stopped catching fish, but because I *couldn't* stop catching them.

We fished like that for two days, Kev and I. Neither of us had any idea how many fish we caught. (Anglers who keep score don't realize how stupid they sound, muttering things like, "I only got seven today, but added to the twenty-seven I got yesterday, that makes thirty-four in all!")

In the evenings we drove the camper over to Lee Lake, a couple of miles south of Burmis alongside Highway 507, and caught fifteen-inch rainbows from our float tubes until cold drove us off the water. Then we'd dump some briquettes in the barbecue, take out a couple of steaks, open the beans, crack two beers, talk about every girl we've ever known and every animal we've ever stalked (sometimes the same quarry). We repeated the ritual every night, a spiritual communion.

* * *

A few summers ago, Kev and I teamed up with Australian guide Will Spry and spent a couple of days fishing at Mike Lamb's place. Mike is a former newspaper reporter and colleague who now runs the River's Edge, a bed-and-breakfast at Burmis. Depending on who you talk to, he's either a legend or a lunatic (in his own mind he's both). While working for the *Lethbridge Herald*, he earned the nickname "Mouth of the South," and I've never heard Mike yell louder than the time I accidentally flipped him out the back of my pickup truck. He landed on his head, and after he'd finished rolling around in the gravel, his wife Laurie noticed that one of his ears was only half-attached. Because there are no hospitals around, we popped into a nearby veterinarian's farm.

"Bite the bullet," he told Mike, sewing his ear back on with a needle and thread. In keeping with the spirit, Mike yelped like a puppy.

Everyone along the Crowsnest knows him, and flyfishers are constantly stopping by his place to shoot the breeze. The front porch of his main fishing lodge (the one with the sauna and the VCR) has nails in the posts to hang your chest waders. You'll have to watch out for the wrens' nest in the bleached steer skull, the birds flying in and out of the eye sockets in morbid fashion.

I like the front porch of his "rustic" lodge even better. It sits atop a grassy knoll between the river and the Canadian Pacific Railway line, so if you don't catch a fish, you can always catch a train. Mike spent months restoring the 1929 cabin, hauling a Franklin fireplace up the hill and hanging an antique thermometer outside the door. The thermometer is the size of a small steelhead, all

Rainbows in the fourteen- to eighteen-inch range predominate in the Crowsnest River, and occasionally you'll hook one a lot bigger.

mercury and numerals—easy to see when you're huddled on the porch in your down mummy bag deciding that it's too cold to get up.

"Come on," Mike will plead, headed down the hill toward the main lodge with Lark, his Brittany spaniel, and you know that the trout down in the mist-cloaked river are starting to stir as well and that the odd one might even be rising to some early-morning midges. Besides, you wouldn't want to miss Mike's sourdough pancakes, slathered in chokecherry syrup squeezed from berries he picks himself.

Yet that particular August—the one when the three of us crashed at Mike's place—was one of the driest on record. All over the province, biologists were worrying about rising water temperatures, and it wasn't only Alberta, either. Will had just come up from the States where the same thing was happening. During the daytime, the Crowsnest fish weren't feeding at all. We could see them bunched up in deep pools, gills pumping to work as much oxygen into their systems as possible. It was disappointing to say the least; even more so because I really wanted Will to have a great trip. A couple of years earlier I'd traveled Down Under to flyfish the Snowy Mountains, and Will had gone out of his way to assure me a good time. The Crow had rendered a dozen tiny rainbows during the daytime, but I knew that Will hadn't flown halfway around the world to catch bait.

"You guys are going to have to change your tactics," Mike told us one afternoon, slumped and perspiring in a tattered armchair on the front porch of the main lodge. "When the weather's like this the big ones won't start feeding till dark." He looked at Will. "Of course, that's when the bears start feeding, too."

That night, after cocktails, Will and I headed downstream; Kev up. A couple of hundred yards below Mike's place, the Crow flows beneath a red bridge and takes a sharp turn, where it gouges away at a gray sandstone cliff. Every so often this erosion causes a piece of the cliff to tumble into the river, creating perfect holding water for trout. Over the years I've gotten to know that fifty-yard stretch intimately, well enough that I know exactly how much line to cast to reach those pockets on the far side, even in the middle of the night. As far as I'm concerned, there are two requisites to fishing in the dark. First, you have to know the water, and second, you have to know that the water holds fish.

We tied on large streamers. Will used a black-and-purple Woolly Bugger, and I tied on a green Zonker, size 4. Although he was only about twenty yards upstream of me, I couldn't see Will at all. I could, however, hear him and knew exactly what he was doing by the sound of his fly line swishing through the air, the sound of his reel surrendering line when he hooked a big rainbow. Human senses dulled by urban living and white noise become sharp in the isolation of a night astream. The ears prick; the head swivels. Think of Cro-Magnon man with his face to the fire and his back to the wilderness, the hiss of a saber-toothed tiger (or, as the case may be, the grunt of a bear) easily distinguishable from the hiss of burning pine.

"Do you think there are any around?" asked Will, his voice amplified in the still air as if he was whispering over my shoulder.

"Probably. But at this time of the year I'm sure they're just black bears. Besides, we're making so much noise there's no way we're going to get close to one."

We fished on. I landed a nice rainbow without ever seeing it, sliding my hands across its slick body like a blind man. I could have turned on my headlamp but chose not to. It would have violated the moment. I hooked a couple of other fish, but they quickly threw the fly. And then, by mutual consent, Will and I decided it was time to head back to Mike's place and the steak dinner that awaited. The headlamp cast a cone of light that we followed along the bank to the bridge and the gravel road. Then we turned the light off, preferring to walk in the dark as we swung around the corner and through the barbed-wire gate into Mike's driveway.

"*Grrrrr!*" Something sprang at us from a clump of willows.

"*Ahhhhh!*" Will and I screamed, simultaneously. We ran in tight circles, Will looking for something to climb, me trying to scamper up his back. Mike Lamb, still growling, dropped on all fours and then started laughing so hard I thought he'd choke.

"I saw your light on the bridge," he said between guffaws. "The big brave fishermen!"

About twenty minutes later, after we'd opened some beers and settled on the porch, Kev walked up the same driveway sopping wet and shivering.

"Fell in, eh?" Mike inquired, laughing anew.

"No," Kev replied. "I *jumped* in." He then told us a story that's become legendary around Mike's place. It goes something like this. Kev hooked a bat. As it flew around and around his body, the fly line coiled around Kev's neck. Finally the bat was flush against his cheek, screeching and flapping and giving Kev a serious case of the heebie-jeebies. Flailing his arms, Kev jumped in the river to "escape," as he put it. Eventually he did, but not until both he and the bat got a thorough soaking. Upon hearing the story, Mike dropped on all fours again, reassuming his bear posture.

"Batman, batman, batman ..." he repeated over and over. I'm sure every guest that's since stayed at his lodge has heard the yarn.

*   *   *

Folklore is nothing new to the Crowsnest Pass, an area rich in legend. One of those legends gave rise to the name itself and has nothing to do with the scavenging black birds. Supposedly many years ago a band of warring Crow Indians camped in the mountain pass. They hid in the rocks and waited for the Blackfoot tribe to approach, but the Blackfoot warriors discovered the Crow first and slaughtered the group. Thereafter they named the area "the nest of the Crows."

By the turn of the century, the Canadian Pacific Railway had built a line into the pass, and it quickly developed into a coal mining region, attracting a colorful mix of workers from places as far afield as Europe and Japan. Those workers in turn championed the arrival of another industry during Alberta's prohibition era from 1916 to 1923—rum-running. Liquor was smuggled in from British Columbia, sometimes Montana. The most notorious rum-runner was Emilio Picariello, otherwise known as Mr. Pick. He started out using Model T Fords with concrete-reinforced bumpers, but later switched to the McLaughlin, nicknamed the "Whiskey Special." Mr. Pick, who also owned the Alberta Hotel (now a Blairmore pharmacy), was found guilty of shooting a policeman and hanged in 1923.

Death and the Crowsnest Pass have often been aligned. During the night of April 29, 1903, a wedge of limestone weighing 900,000,000 *tons* slid off the face of Turtle Mountain and roared down into the valley. The rock partially destroyed the village of Frank, killing an estimated seventy people while they slept and barricading the Crowsnest River. Eventually the limestone was dynamited to open a channel for the river, but there is still a small lake at the base of Turtle Mountain. The lake holds rainbows up to seven pounds and is best fished in late summer from a float tube. However, the lunar shoreline and looming mountainside, scooped away like a half-eaten container of licorice ice cream, can be unnerving to say the least.

Tragedy struck the Crowsnest again in 1914, when an explosion at the Hillcrest Mine killed 189 men and boys. All the coal mines along the Crowsnest

Kevin "Batman" Watson and a Crowsnest River rainbow.

are now closed, but flyrodders can still see reminders at several spots. Just below Hillcrest is a stretch known locally as the Tipple Run, where a decaying coal tipple (the place at a mine entrance where coal cars are emptied and filled) overlooks the river from the rim of Highway 3 to the east.

In an attempt to thwart urban decay (the area's economy has been depressed for decades), in 1979 the communities of Bellevue, Hillcrest, Frank, Blairmore, and Coleman merged to become the Crowsnest Municipality, the third largest municipal landmass in the province. Still, don't get the idea the Crowsnest is overrun. Most of the housing is clustered along a narrow swath of Highway 3. You don't need to wander far to find grizzly and black bears, wolves, elk, moose, wild turkeys, and mule and white-tailed deer—even mink. Blue and purple wild lupine is common along the roadsides; farther downstream, as the montane forest flattens into grassland, the brown-eyed susans gaze across prairie fields. Strangest of all is the yellow locoweed, a tall, clustered plant that causes mental disturbances in livestock. Personally, I've never found cows altogether sane to begin with. Any animal that needs to be nudged with a bumper to clear out of the way and then looks amorously at the truck as it passes, is already loco in my book.

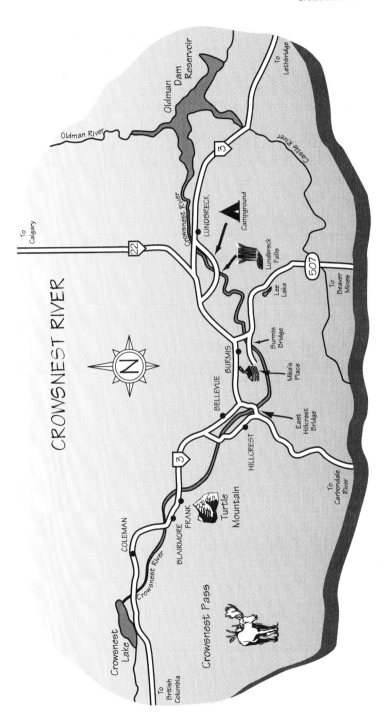

When You Go

Getting There

If you're driving east from British Columbia or north from Kalispell, Montana, get on Highway 3, which runs through Crowsnest Pass and parallels the Crowsnest River for much of its thirty-mile length. An alternate route from Montana—and the best one if you're *east* of the Rockies—is to follow Interstate 15 north to the Canadian border and continue north on Highway 4 to the junction with Highway 3 at Lethbridge. Turn west and drive about eighty miles to the Crowsnest.

The easiest route from Calgary is to drive south on Highway 2 for about ninety miles, turn west on Highway 3, and drive for about forty miles to the river.

River Access

The Crowsnest River rises in the Rockies near the continental divide and ends at the Oldman Dam Reservoir. Along the way it flows through a lot of private land. Fortunately, more than a dozen bridges provide convenient access, and those bridges are never far from Highway 3. The best fishing is below Hillcrest. Bridges to watch for are at East Hillcrest (Passburg), Burmis Lake, and Highway 507. Farther downstream, around and below Lundbreck Falls, there's plenty of public access, but the river tends to get crowded, particularly on weekends. The Highway 3 bridge also provides good access to this stretch.

Equipment

For fly rods, I favor a lighter rod on the Crow than I do, say, on the Bow. I've had some great days fishing the runs and riffles of the Crow with an eight-foot, three-weight rod, particularly during a hatch of small insects. But don't forget to pack a five- or six-weight rod as well. You'll need it when the wind's blowing (which happens more often than not along the Crow) or when you're casting weighted nymphs or streamers. A heavier rod also makes it easier to turn over bulky salmonfly imitations. If the wind's *really* howling, head for the stretch of river just downstream of the East Hillcrest (Passburg) bridge.

The Crow snakes through sheltered forest there, and you shouldn't have much trouble finding spots to cast.

Bring the same clothing and accessories you'd take on any Alberta trip, remembering to be prepared for any weather at any time of the year.

Fly Patterns

Without a doubt, the Crow is one of the most fertile trout streams in the Rockies. One analysis revealed nine varieties of stoneflies, eleven varieties of mayflies, and four different caddisflies. There are golden stones, yellow sallies (little yellow stoneflies), lime sallies (little green stoneflies), blue-winged olives, March browns, pale morning duns, western green drakes, small western green drakes, red quills, western blue duns, American grannom, green sedge, October caddis, crane flies, midges, grasshoppers, beetles, cinnamon-colored ants, black-colored ants, and ants in your pants. I'm still waiting for the Crow to offer up a new species of insect, some freakish variant that has evolved in the gene-laden soup.

Patterns? Use your imagination. Royal Wulffs, Trudes, and other small attractors work well near the river's headwaters below Crowsnest Lake. The river is little more than a creek there, meandering through a wide valley thick with willows and brush, and the trout rarely exceed twelve inches. I'm not a huge fan of this section—grizzly and black bears are—and the only time I fish it is when the lower river is off-color. Farther downstream, below the Crowsnest Municipality, you're going to want the usual array of mayfly, caddis, and stonefly patterns, both nymphs and dries.

The fish are particularly fond of nymphs with peacock herl, such as Prince and Pheasant Tail nymphs, sizes 12 to 18. Other good bets are San Juan Worms, Bitch Creeks, Brooks' Golden Stone, and Montana nymphs (sizes 4 to 10). For dries, I carry a smattering of Elk Hair and Goddard Caddis (sizes 10 to 18), Adams, Irresistibles and other generic mayfly imitations (sizes 12 to 18), and Letort Hoppers and Stimulators, sizes 6 to 14, the larger sizes to imitate adult salmonflies.

That said, my favorite pattern, hands-down, for the middle and lower Crowsnest is still the Lime Trude. Depending on the size, I find it imitates everything from yellow and lime sallies to PMDs. Rainbows seem especially attracted to the white downwing. For years, this pattern has outperformed all other dry flies at the annual One Fly Contest on Wyoming's Snake River. The rules limit each contestant to one fly all day; if the angler loses or breaks the fly off, that's it. A couple of years ago I had a chance to meet innovative fly tier and author Gary LaFontaine, and he told me his favorite attractor pattern over the years has been the Trude. (Remember, this is a guy who actually donned scuba gear and spent hours at the bottom of rivers observing feeding trout; when he talks, I listen.)

For those frustrating early- and late-season midge hatches, I carry a few Griffith's Gnats and Renegades, sizes 18 to 22. And, finally, I never fish the Crow without streamers, particularly Woolly Buggers, in the usual variety of colors and sizes. The Spruce Fly and Mylar Mickey Finn can also be effective in sizes 6 to 10, particularly during hot weather in late August or early September.

Seasons and Tactics

I've already described the mid-May salmonfly hatch in detail, so I won't repeat myself here. Prior to the *Pteronarcys* emergence, the midges and blue-winged olives start hatching in April, the March browns several weeks later. Nevertheless, dry-fly fishing can be spotty because of the unsettled weather. The best bet is to fish weighted nymphs through deeper runs and pools, keeping in mind that the low, clear water will make the trout especially wary. Early spring and late fall are the only times of the year when I find myself using exceptionally long leaders (that means fourteen-foot leaders to me) and 6X tippets on the Crow. The rest of the season, nine- to twelve-foot leaders and 5X will work fine for dries, nine-foot leaders and 3X or 4X for nymphs.

No sooner do the salmonflies stop hatching than the golden stones and sallies begin, lasting well into July. This is also when mayfly emergences start to overlap one another. PMD and green drake fishing can be spectacular from late June into August. Watch for the former to start coming off in the afternoons, the latter toward the evenings, particularly during rainy weather. Caddis hatch throughout the summer evenings as well, and casting to riseforms after sunset is a good way to hook big fish.

August and September can be fickle months on the Crowsnest. As the water drops, the trout tend to become more selective, and while you'll still hook plenty of smaller fish, catching the twenty-inchers requires stealth and sneaky tactics. Try using streamers just before and after dark and early in the morning. Don't be afraid to tie on something gaudy, either. I know one Crowsnest fly-rodder who catches trophy rainbows in the middle of the day each summer using Spruce Flies and Mylar Mickey Finns! On windy days, watch for grass-hoppers blowing onto the water. One of the best stretches for hopper fishing is along the buff sandstone cliffs near Lundbreck. The only brown trout in the Crowsnest are downstream of twenty-five-foot Lundbreck Falls (a natural bar-rier); fishing to them with big orange- or yellow-bodied Stimulators or Letort Hoppers can work well. Late summer is also a good time to fish crane fly imi-tations below the falls. Just before sunrise is the best time of day.

In the fall, the vivid autumn backdrop, red and yellow and gold and rust, is the perfect accompaniment to the excellent midge and blue-winged olive fishing. The mountains are often capped with snow, and the flyfishing is best after midday and into the evening, when the river will have warmed up enough to make the insects active.

Special Regulations

There are numerous special regulations governing the Crowsnest—far too many to list here. Please read the regulations carefully to avoid embarrassment at the hands of a fish-and-game officer. Seasonal closures and slot-limits apply to much of the river, but at the time of this writing, the portion between the East Hillcrest (Passburg) bridge and Lundbreck Falls and the section between the Highway 3 and Cowley bridges are open all year. Of course, *open* is a rel-ative word—large tracts of the river freeze over during the winter, though warm springs do keep some runs ice-free year-round.

Places to Stay and Eat

There are several good motels and restaurants in Blairmore and Coleman. For specific information, contact the Crowsnest Pass Chamber of Commerce (403-562-8776). If you don't mind straying a few miles west along Highway 3, my personal favorite is the Inn on the Border (Box 426, Blairmore, Alta., Canada, T0K 0E0; 403-563-3101). It literally straddles the Alberta-British Columbia border, and adjacent Summit Lake stocked with cutthroat trout (you'll need a B.C. license to fish it, though). I've been told the restaurant's kitchen is in

Alberta and the dining room in B.C. The men's john appears to be the unofficial dividing line, and the thought has often occurred to me that I might be sitting on an Alberta throne but washing my hands in B.C. Try the prime rib sandwich with a Big Rock Traditional Ale. There's always a good selection of homemade desserts on the blackboard as well. After you've eaten, walk over to the lake with a float tube and fish until dark with small nymphs or dries.

If you're into the bed-and-breakfast scene, the Crowsnest has some dandies. I've already talked about Mike Lamb's place, the River's Edge (Box 71, Bellevue, Alta., Canada, T0K 0C0; 403-564-4271 or 403-283-6545). Another good one is The Bedside Manor (Box 1088, Blairmore, Alta., Canada, T0K 0E0; 403-628-3954). Provincial campgrounds are numerous in the area. The most popular one with visiting anglers is Lundbreck Falls, where late-night b.s. sessions between flyfishers are commonplace throughout the summer.

Guides and Outfitters

Vic Bergman has been fishing the Crow for most of his life and probably knows the river better than anyone. He also runs a fly shop across Highway 3 from some of the best runs. Contact him at The Crowsnest Angler (22614 27th Ave., Box 400, Bellevue, Alta., Canada, T0K 1C0; 403-564-4333). I also strongly recommend Bob Lowe at Kingfisher Guides' Service (Box 656, Pincher Creek, Alta., Canada, T0K 1W0; 403-627-5584).

Other Attractions

As you might expect, Crowsnest Pass has several noteworthy tourist attractions relating to the region's coal mining history. The best is the Frank Slide Interpretive Centre, which not only details the 1903 disaster, but also gives a pretty good account of the area's history. Watch for the turn-off on the north side of Highway 3 at Frank. A few miles farther east, also alongside the highway, are the remains of the Leitch Collieries, a provincial historic site that's worth a look.

5
Castle River

"Buddy" is a dog, a mongrel, a character, and one of the most astute companions I've ever fished with.

Yes, with.

Buddy, you see, is gifted. What he lacks in adroitness—namely, the prehensile thumb and opposing fingers needed to grip a fly rod—he more than compensates for with know-how. Hook a runt, and Buddy will turn his shiny black nose in the air, cough, and coolly scratch himself behind an ear. Hook a trophy, and Buddy will pant, leaning over the edge of the boat and eyeing the fish like a middle linebacker sizing up a quarterback.

"I've never seen anything like it," I told guide Bob Lowe, who was jack-knifed over the oars as our raft bobbed along on the silty Castle River. Buddy, a rumpled mix of schnauzer, poodle, and terrier, had been anticipating my every move. I swung left, he walked right, gingerly avoiding the loose fly line coiled on the deck. I swung right, he sauntered to the back of a pontoon, giving me a look through that tousled brow of his that seemed to say, Go ahead, but I've been here a thousand times, and I guarantee there isn't a fish under that bank you're casting to!

Buddy anticipated strikes. Just as a good flyfisher knows when a drift looks particularly promising—when the grip tightens and the neck hunches— Buddy knew when to pay attention and when to sniff at the cooler. Truth is, I'd taken a liking to Buddy, and I'd also taken a liking to Bob, who guided on the Bow River for over a decade before swapping watersheds and heading south. Bob has a ruddy complexion and puckered mouth; his freckled arms are as strong as you'd expect after years of pulling on oars. Beneath the ever-present sunglasses, his eyes twinkle—the single trait he shares with Buddy, who is black-haired with a white muzzle and legs.

"Buddy's been doing float trips for a dozen years," Bob said, slipping the raft into an eddy to roll a cigarette. "He used to spend hours lying on the back of a pontoon, but sooner or later he'd fall asleep, and the next thing you know he'd be swimming."

Bob opened a fly box and handed me a red-bodied Stimulator. The morning's fishing had been slow on this river, which flowed briskly as it wound through the foothills of southwestern Alberta. Although it was July, the water still had an opaque cloudiness from the late run-off. I dipped the end of my four-piece rod into the river; the tip-top vanished before the final two-foot tip section was fully submerged.

Bob reached for the oars again and yanked the raft back into a tongue of current. The water caught the sunlight, held it, and threw it back into the air as a thousand blinding flashes. In the middle of all that light, the Stimulator floated along the surface. Buddy tensed. An oar creaked. A rainbow struck. The foot-long trout tumbled across the surface, water droplets spraying from its body. Leaning over the pontoon, I slid my hand down the leader, took the fly between my thumb and forefinger, and twisted. The trout plopped back into the river and darted away. I turned to look at Buddy, but he was looking the other way, scratching himself. Talk about a critic.

"The big ones just don't seem hungry," Bob surmised. I'd caught half a dozen rainbows and cutthroats between six and twelve inches. Nothing to boast about; better than nothing. Bob was apologetic, but I told him not to worry about it. Earlier that morning I'd yanked the fly away from a couple of larger rainbows, maybe eighteen inches. In fact, if anyone had reason to be ticked off, it was Bob. His two-person raft is designed to shoot rapids and turn quickly. As a result, there's not a lot of room between the elevated casting seat and the rowing seat level with the pontoons. The back of Bob's head, as fate would have it, was flush with my right elbow.

"Sorry, Bob," I'd say, clubbing him yet again as I leaned into a cast downstream in front of the boat.

"No problem." The next thing you know he'd be telling me to reel in and hang on as the raft jolted through a rough stretch, with Buddy standing stiff-legged and solemn. Even as far downstream as we were floating, below Secondary Highway 507, the Castle shouldn't be underestimated. Its rocks are sharp; its currents contradictory. No wonder Buddy had stopped falling asleep on the pontoons.

* * *

The Castle and Bob go back a long way, back to a childhood spent with a creel slung over a shoulder, back to a childhood spent with a big toe dangling in the river beneath a big tree.

"My dad and I started fishing here when I was seven or eight years old," Bob told me. In those days, catch-and-release was something you did to tadpoles, not trout. As Bob put it, "We were seriously into harvesting then." But times change. And people. And attitudes. Although the regulations still permit the killing of trout on the Castle, most anglers toss them back.

"I really think this area has the potential to be the next flyfishing mecca," Bob said, his creel long since retired, a wicker receptacle for memories. Potential? Some would argue the mecca already exists.

The Castle drainage actually consists of two forks and the river formed by their merger. The South Castle, the larger of the two, is primarily a cutthroat fishery. It rises just east of Sage Mountain, coursing through the layered strata of the Rockies and plunging northward past Table Mountain. Some of the trout are huge: the provincial record cutthroat was caught in the South Castle in 1988, a 9 lb., 9 oz. brute that must have parted the waters as it made its first run. What I would have given to see its monstrous silver body against

Bob Lowe and flyfishing critic Buddy, ready for a float on the Castle River.

the jade- and copper-colored cobblestones; the fish must have been decades old to grow that size in the frigid alpine headwaters.

A few miles west—a couple of valleys over—is the West Castle River, smaller and more popular with flyfishers. It, too, holds plenty of cutthroats, along with rainbows, bulls, and mountain whitefish. Between the two river valleys, among the ramparts and conifers of Barnaby Ridge, are alpine lakes stocked with golden trout. The West Castle and South Castle roughly parallel one another until they converge northwest of Beaver Mines Lake, forming the Castle River. From there the river exits the mountains and enters the foothills. This is the sprawling, undulating countryside of mixed-grass ranches fenced by sandstone and shale, of a smothering blue sky, of grizzly bears and cattle sharing the same meadow. The area encompasses some of the most valuable wildlife habitat in North America. So valuable, in fact, that biologists have given the mountainous country between Montana's Bob Marshall Wilderness and Alberta's Crowsnest Pass a special designation: the Crown of the Continent Ecosystem. Bighorn sheep, wolves, elk, deer, wolverines— the abundance of mammals is incredible. I've seen moose loping across a cow pasture, dark brown and conspicuous.

I've also seen a white-tailed doe and her fawn frolicking in a field covered by sticky purple geraniums. I watched the pair for ten minutes from fifty yards away. The fawn, tawny with white spots, pounced on unseen adversaries with stiff legs, pogo-stick-style. The mother watched, flicking her tail anxiously. I could tell she wanted to coax the youngster back into the protective aspens, nature's crib. A Richardson's ground squirrel spotted me prone in the field before the deer did; when its shrill whistle announced my presence, the deer froze. Who says animals can't talk?

Ground squirrels and gophers, incidentally, come from different scientific families, but the names are used interchangeably. The true prairie dog is rare in Canada but common on the American plains. In the late 1890s American rancher Morace Quinby decided to get rich by killing prairie dogs and shipping the dressed bodies to eastern markets. When diners opened the menus at fashionable New York restaurants, the "mountain squirrel" entrée caught many an eye. Not until a buyer ventured west to increase the supply did anyone figure out what Quinby was up to (by then he had plenty of competition). "Mountain squirrel" was quietly taken off the menus; few diners were the wiser.

I imagine a few Richardson's ground squirrels have been eaten along the Castle drainage. By foraging grizzlies, whose hillside excavations pock the valley, and by Rocky Mountain hillbillies, reputed to carry XXX jugs. The remote foothills and mountains southwest of Pincher Creek have long attracted a different breed: beware chainsaws and coyotes howling in the night.

* * *

Bob was into his fifth or sixth cigarette by the time the fishing began to pick up. We'd entered a slate-gray canyon and had come across a dubious pair of anglers jigging for bull trout. Still using the red-bodied Stimulator, I caught two decent cutthroats in quick succession, the latter with an open wound across its back, the legacy of a sharp beak or glancing talon. Then I caught a sixteen-inch rainbow, a trout that lurked behind a submerged boulder, black and menacing. The sky, too, was dire. A bank of dark clouds congealed to the west, and Bob and I exchanged knowing glances as the sun disappeared and the first gust of wind brushed the water. Within five minutes hailstones half an inch in diameter plunged into the river, frozen meteorites that threatened

Bob Lowe fishes the Castle River, which flows through some of the most valuable wildlife habitat in North America.

to shatter my graphite rod, which I'd foolishly left on the raft while we sought cover beneath a cottonwood tree. Leaves, many still attached to small branches, were knocked to the ground. Buddy, who hadn't made a sound through the worst of the storm, took two steps out from beneath the tree and had a hailstone bounce four feet off his noggin. Without a whimper, he retreated and tucked his head in the crook of my knee.

"He's seen worse," Bob deadpanned. Somehow, I believed him. The storm moved east, its shadow sweeping across the prairie, and we returned to the raft. The water had come up at least two inches; it was dirty and filled with flotsam. In the eddies, hailstones gathered and tinkled like ice in a cocktail glass. Even before Bob told me, I knew the fishing was done. No matter. We were close to the take-out anyway, and Bob used the rest of the float to talk about the Castle and its environs.

"You can't float this river in anything but rubber," he said. "I know. I've tried it." Years ago, Bob attempted to navigate the Castle in a Mackenzie drift boat. Bob came through unscathed, but the same couldn't be said of the boat. "This," he continued, "is a river where people can get themselves in trouble."

By summer's end, the Castle water level drops to a point where Bob won't even float the river in a raft; after that it's strictly a walk-and-wade proposition. When he can float the river, Bob said that flyfishing clients usually land about a dozen trout between sixteen and eighteen inches in an average day. The biggest rainbow he's ever seen taken from the lower Castle was twenty-five inches—an exceptional fish, even by Bow River standards.

*   *   *

Mid-August. The Castle had dropped as much as Bob had predicted a month earlier, but Mike Lamb and I decided to give it a go anyway in our Metzeler inflatables. Mike, you'll recall, is the "Mouth of the South" of Crowsnest River infamy. The Metzeler is a small, orange, one-man raft (there are larger models as well), and although it's actually designed as a tender to be towed behind a yacht, Mike and I bought ours for float trips. We decided to tackle the lower Castle below the confluence with Mill Creek. Mike knows a rancher there who had given us permission to put-in on his property. Even that far downstream, we both realized that we'd probably have to portage around the worst whitewater.

On the way to the put-in west of Pincher Creek, we drove past the Cowley Ridge Wind Electric Project, where fifty-two colossal turbines (each eighty feet tall with twenty-six-foot blades) stand testament to the winds that roar over the mountains and onto the plains—some of the strongest in the country. Fortunately for Mike and I, the blades were idle that morning, the megawatts on hold. Wind-generated electricity is commendable in principle, but I'd hate to be the one swearing at my toaster during the doldrums.

The Pincher Creek area is rife with oddities. The town itself received its name when a Mounted Police patrol apparently found a pair of pincers—used for trimming horses' hooves—along the namesake creek. One of the Castle River tributaries is called Screwdriver Creek, and I've always wondered if the same klutz that dropped the pincers left a trail of tools scattered across the foothills.

Mike and I inflated the rafts with an electric air pump, attaching it to the truck battery. Then we changed into our fishing gear, loaded the boats with coolers and day packs, and carried them to the river's edge, one at a time. The water was clear. I tied a size 8 Lime Trude to the end of a twelve-foot leader. The Metzelers are impractical to fish from, so Mike and I stopped and worked all the good water from shore. We caught fish immediately—good-sized rainbows

Mike Lamb prepares to tackle the lower Castle River in a Metzeler one-man raft.

that hung beneath the seams along the bank and behind the midstream boulders. About forty-five minutes into the trip, one of those boulders did Mike in. We were floating through a rock garden, dodging left and right, when Mike wedged an oar on the upstream side of a boulder, snapping it in half. He shouted, and I glanced across the river and saw him waving the amputated splinter in the air. Somehow, Mike managed to maneuver the raft through the rest of the rapids, and I towed him to shore.

"Well, I guess that's the end of our trip," he said. I thought this over for a moment before replying.

"No, I guess that's the end of *your* trip. I'm going on."

Fine, Mike said, just as long as I ferried him across the river so he could walk back to his truck, less than a mile upstream. There was an old road on a small hill overlooking the river, and Mike marked the location so he could drive back later and pick up his raft. (We'd shuttled my truck to the take-out, so I'd carry on as planned and drive back to Mike's place that evening.)

"Good luck," Mike said, setting out across a meadow. "I'll have the steaks thawed out and ready to go when you get back tonight."

Good-sized rainbows hang along the bank and behind boulders and sweepers in the West Castle River.

The trip took on a different character once Mike was gone. Suddenly, the importance of successfully negotiating the rapids, ledges, and chutes hit home—if my raft flipped now and I wound up swimming, the result could be disastrous. While in Mike's company the prospects of disaster had been secondary to the prospects of catching fish. Now the reverse was true, and it changed the way I regarded the water. A boulder was no longer something to cast a fly behind, but a lurking foe; a pool was no longer a trout repository, but a respite between rapids.

As I viewed the river differently, the peripheral scenery shifted focus as well. The sandstone cliffs, glowing in the tilted golden light of late afternoon, were an eroded reminder of the river's force. Hoodoo rock columns pierced the valley walls, the remnant fingers of a geological hand sculpted by wind and water. I floated past a great blue heron rookery, the tangled nests perched high in the skeletal branches of a dead cottonwood grove. I floated past an Indian teepee on the bank. I floated past a decaying pump house, its weathered planks peeling and blistered. The natural elements touched—shaped—everything around me. I lost track of time, stopping periodically to catch fifteen-inch rainbows, hoisting them in the net from water as cold as the air was hot.

In *Desert Solitaire*, naturalist Edward Abbey, floating down the Colorado River with a companion, writes: "Why, we ask ourselves, floating onward in effortless peace deeper into Eden, why not go on like this forever?"

My trip had been far from effortless; still, prolonging the float seemed like a good idea that day on the Castle. Regrettably, "forever" only took me as far as the take-out and my truck, where someone had tucked a note under a windshield wiper blade:

> *Chris—*
> *I got treed by a grizz for 45 minutes—no shit. I hope your day went better. I'll tell you more about the bear later. See ya for steak.*
> *Mike*
> *P.S. I musta left your pants at the raft.*

The bear, Mike said later, had been on the other side of that meadow he'd set out to cross on the way back to his pickup. And although the grizzly didn't threaten him, Mike said climbing a cottonwood seemed appropriate at the time. Eventually, the bear wandered off and disappeared over a rise, deeper into an Eden of its own choosing.

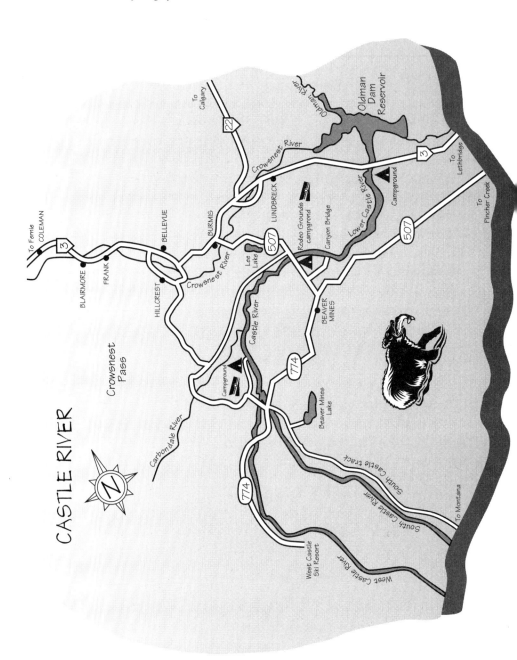

CASTLE RIVER

When You Go

Getting There

From Montana, follow Interstate 15 north to the Canadian border. Continue north on Highway 4 to the junction with Highway 3 at Lethbridge. Turn west and drive about seventy-five miles to the junction with Secondary Highway 507. Head south, and after about eight miles you'll come to the highway bridge across the Castle River. To reach the junction of the South Castle and West Castle Rivers, continue south for another three miles; then take the turnoff into Beaver Mines along Secondary Highway 774. The two rivers join about ten miles past the town.

To reach the Castle River from Calgary, drive south on Highway 2 for about ninety miles; then turn west on Highway 3 and drive for about thirty-five miles to the junction with Secondary Highway 507. From there follow the directions given above.

River Access

Below the forest reserve boundary (about a mile and a half upstream of the Castle's confluence with the Carbondale River) the Castle River flows through private land. Some ranchers will grant permission and some won't; it never hurts to ask. Public access to this stretch is possible at the Highway 507 and Canyon Bridges and at two campgrounds: the Rodeo Grounds just off Highway 507 south of the river and another upstream of where the Castle starts backing up before entering Oldman Dam Reservoir, west of Pincher Creek.

Accessing the Castle in the forest reserve is a breeze; basically you can fish anywhere geography permits. Secondary Highway 774 follows the West Castle all the way to the river's namesake ski area, and a brutally rough 4x4 track continues past that point. You can access the South Castle River from the Secondary Highway 774 bridge just above the confluence of the two forks. There's also a dubious 4x4 track that follows the river for several miles south of Beaver Mines Lake. (A word of caution: I won't even drive this in my beat-up truck; best to stick with horses, mountain bikes, ATVs, or hiking boots.) Also keep in mind that this valley has one of the province's highest grizzly populations.

For flyfishers planning their own float trips, my advice is to keep the boat on the trailer unless you *really* know the river and what you're doing. Even on the lower Castle, some sections, such as the steeply-walled notch downstream of the Canyon Bridge, are unnavigable in fishing craft of any sort. As Mike Lamb's rafting incident aptly illustrates, boaters can quickly get in trouble on the Castle. At the very least, you'll require a durable raft with a solid rowing frame. Water levels permitting, the best full-day float, albeit a *very* long one, is to put in at the Carbondale Campground and take out at the Rodeo Grounds Campground just east of Secondary Highway 507. Before floating check with the Crowsnest Angler fly shop (number below) for a condition report.

Equipment

Size wise, the Castle is one of the larger streams in southwestern Alberta, especially as it exits the forest reserve and picks up water from a handful of notable tributaries, including the Carbondale River, Screwdriver Creek, and Beaver Mines Creek. With that in mind (and taking into account that the wind can really blow here as well), I usually opt for at least a five-weight rod along the lower reaches. Upstream I'll occasionally pull the four-weight out of its tube. Along the West Castle, which is much smaller and tighter, a three-weight works just fine.

As far as the Castle and South Castle are concerned, leader length and tippet size aren't as big a deal as they are on rivers such as the nearby Crowsnest, where the trout tend to be fussier. I usually flyfish with nine- to twelve-foot leaders with 4X tippets. On the West Castle, where the hatches tend to be more pronounced and the natural insects smaller, bring along some 5X and 6X as well.

Come equipped with the same clothing and accessories you'd take anywhere else in southern Alberta, keeping in mind that the Castle and its tributaries drain mountainous country where the weather is extremely unpredictable.

Fly Patterns

Big flies. That's the rule of thumb on the Castle (with the exception of the West Castle fork, which I'll deal with separately in a moment). By big, I mean sizes 6 to 10 attractor dry flies—things like Trudes, red-bodied Stimulators, Letort Hoppers, Royal and Grizzly Wulffs, and guide Bob Lowe's "Elvis," which is basically a Trude with a yellow calf tail down-wing. (Fish it as you would any other dry fly; then when the Elvis starts to drag, yank it beneath the surface and strip it back toward you, streamer style. You can do the same thing with tightly-hackled Stimulators and other streamlined dry flies, which is one of the reasons I like to fish them so much.)

I rarely nymph on the Castle, for no other reason than that I've rarely needed to. Occasionally I'll tie a small Beadhead Pheasant Tail or Hare's Ear on as a dropper beneath the dry fly, attaching it to the bend of the dry fly's hook with a twelve- to eighteen-inch leader. If the water's dirty from rain or run-off and nymphing is your only option, try a Brooks' Golden Stone or Montana Nymph (sizes 4 to 10).

The West Castle, particularly for several miles upstream of its confluence with the South Castle, is a bit more demanding. Fishing pressure can be heavy; so can the hatches. Smaller attractors still work well there, but go prepared with some mayfly and caddisfly imitations, too. I suggest Elk Hair and Goddard caddis in sizes 10 to 18, and Adams, Irresistibles, and Borger Yarn Wing Duns in sizes 12 to 18.

Regardless of where you fish along the Castle or its feeder streams, if it's bottom-hugging bull trout you're after, then you're going to need streamers. Best bets are black Woolly Buggers, Zonkers, and Clouser Minnows, sizes 2 to 6. I'm not a big fan of flyfishing for bull trout, the piscine equivalent of a garbage scow. Still, I know a few anglers who fervently stalk them, convinced that the bulls' nativeness to Alberta's streams is reason enough.

Seasons and Tactics

Unfortunately (for the flyfisher), the Castle watershed doesn't open to angling until June 1. The result is that even when the magic day rolls around, the river is typically in flood. Run-off varies according to the mountain snowpack and spring rain, but don't expect the Castle to become really fishable until July. Sometimes that's even pushing things a bit. Fact is, the Castle drains some of the highest and most isolated terrain in the province, and I'd rather put up with a lengthy run-off than see a dam constructed along this magnificent watercourse.

There's an unpredictable emergence of golden stoneflies on the Castle either just before or during run-off. The significance of this unheralded event to the flyfisher, come July, is that the trout seem to remember the large naturals weeks after they've disappeared. As soon as the water starts clearing, I use big attractor dries like yellow-bodied Stimulators, Lime Trudes, and Letort Hoppers. As the summer progresses I stick with the same patterns but never hesitate to experiment with different colors: red bodies are a favorite. Bob Lowe is convinced big flies are the way to go on the Castle all season long. For one thing, summers are brief along the continental spine, and by the time the water clears, Bob figures the Castle River rainbows and cutthroats are hell bent on eating every sizable bug that comes along.

Flyfish the Castle the same way you'd fish any other boisterous freestone stream. There's lots of great holding water, mile after mile of pools, gravelly riffles, flats, undercut banks, midstream boulders, and tumbled trees. Come autumn, my favorite section is that between the river's confluence with Beaver Mines Creek and Highway 3. As water levels fall farther upstream, the biggest trout tend to congregate there. The tributaries entering the Castle below the forest reserve boundary help keep the flow rate up and the temperature down.

Special Regulations

The season runs from June 1 to October 31 upstream of Highway 3. Please note that bull trout are protected throughout Alberta and must be released. The regulations downstream of Highway 3 are the same as for the Oldman Dam Reservoir, but this section is near-stagnant and of little interest to the flyrodder in search of flowing water.

Places to Stay and Eat

The nearest town of note is Pincher Creek, two miles south of Highway 3 and several miles east of the lower Castle River. There are a handful of good motels and restaurants there. There are also a few bed-and-breakfasts scattered throughout the area. Contact the Pincher Creek Chamber of Commerce (Box 2287, Pincher Creek, Alta., Canada, T0K 1W0; 403-627-5199). If you're into camping, you've come to the right river. The forest reserve has several provincial campgrounds, and you can camp almost anywhere you want

Ian Thomson on the North Raven River.

A Red Deer River goldeye.

Ron Manz with North Ram River cutthroat.

The Oldman River.

Prairie Creek.

The Highwood River.

The Crowsnest River.

Ian Thomson on the West Castle River.

Dave Brown and Julie with Elk River cutthroat.

Lower Bow River with Calgary skyline in background.

Mike Lamb on the upper Bow River.

along the Castle and its forks if you don't mind roughing it. Along the lower river I'd recommend the Rodeo Grounds Campground.

Guides and Outfitters

Bob Lowe has fished here since he was old enough to do up his own fly—never mind tie one on. Reach him at Kingfisher Guides' Service (Box 656, Pincher Creek, Alta., Canada, T0K 1W0; 403-627-5584). Bob also offers guided trips on the Waterton and the St. Mary, both good trout fisheries in the same corner of the province. Vic Bergman at the Crowsnest Angler (Box 400, Bellevue, Alta., Canada, T0K 1C0; 403-564-4333) also arranges Castle River trips.

Other Attractions

Much of the Castle River watershed is remote; the most noteworthy attraction is the arresting landscape it flows through. The scenery alone, a staircase of plateaus and foothills ascending the front range of the Rockies, is worth the trip. If possible, try to visit the Pincher Creek Museum and Kootenai Brown Historical Park—it features an impressive array of log buildings dating back to the 1880s. For buildings of a different sort, the town's Crystal Village is constructed of over 200,000 glass telephone insulators set in cement. The miniature hamlet consists of ten buildings. Tacky, but interesting. If you're still curious about the area's natural history, see the "Other Attractions" listing under the previous chapter on the nearby Crowsnest River.

6
Oldman River

My father electrocuted me once, though he claims it was unintentional. It happened just downstream of the Livingstone Gap along the Oldman River. I'd been rigging up at the tailgate of my four-wheel-drive, while Dad had been watching a couple of kids and an older angler lean over the fence near the edge of a bluff to spot the river about thirty feet below. I finished doing up my boot laces, checked to see if the truck doors were locked for a third time, and sauntered over to join him.

"It's okay," he said, gesturing to the thin wire strands of the electric fence. "I saw a kid grab one. It must be turned off."

Now, normally when I come across an electric fence in cattle country, I don't take any chances. On New Zealand's South Island "hot" fences are commonplace. A guide there explained to me several years ago that the best way to cross one is to push down on the top strand with the cork grip on your fly rod. Cork is an insulator, and once the wire is low enough, you just straddle the fence and hop over. Keep in mind, however, that even the simplest undertaking can occasionally take a disastrous turn. If the wire strand should slip out from underneath the cork grip, you could be doing Jerry Lewis impersonations for the rest of your life.

But Dad had said the fence was turned off, and I believed him. I wrapped my left hand around the top wire and gripped hard. Nothing happened for an instant, then my arm spasmed involuntarily, as if I'd been shot in the wrist with a .357 Magnum.

"Christ!" I screamed, jumping back from the fence. "I've been electrocuted!" Dad, thinking I was putting him on, started laughing. Of course that didn't go over too well.

"*You* grab it," I told him, but he was much too smart to test my veracity where voltage was concerned. A marble-sized lump formed on the inside of my wrist, just above the watch strap. Knotted muscle. "You know," I lectured Dad a little later, when I'd calmed down, "I could have had a heart attack or something."

"That's all right," he replied earnestly. "I know CPR."

* * *

Funny, but the cork grip of a fly rod has never insulated me from the jolt that jumps up my arm and into my psyche each time a big trout swipes my dry fly from the surface of a swift-moving stream. If that dry fly happens to be a grasshopper imitation and that stream happens to be the Oldman River, the combination can be sublime. Hoppers thrive in arid, grassy country, and the Oldman coils like a blue snake as it crosses some of the driest terrain in southern Alberta. The first hoppers start appearing along the river in April, their vermilion-colored bodies brazen against the lackluster vegetation awaiting the May cloudbursts that will wash away the residue of winter.

The grass stalks crackled underfoot as Mike Lamb and I poked around the Oldman below the Summerview Bridge a few Aprils ago. The river was low, its freestone bottom coated in yellow-green algae yet to be scoured by run-off. And although we kicked up grasshoppers, their blurred wings clicking as they leapt ahead of us, the wind wasn't strong enough to blow them onto the water.

"Looks like we'll have to improvise," Mike said, tying on a chartreuse streamer that I couldn't identify. (Suffice it to say that it was big, gaudy, and at the top of Mike's fly box, which is probably why he chose it.) I opted for a San Juan Worm, orange indicator, and several strands of twist-on Larva Lace. I crossed the sixty-foot wide river along a gravel shelf, walked upstream a few yards, and began casting into the elbow of a sharp corner. The river yielded a fifteen-inch mountain whitefish on the first drift. It throbbed at the end of the line as whitefish are wont to do; reeling it in was like dragging a brick across the streambed. I caught four more whitefish and then decided to venture downstream to see if I couldn't locate a trout.

When I caught up with Mike, he was fishing across the river from a sandstone cliff, casting the streamer so it darted along a series of submerged shale ledges, which showed up as knuckles in the translucent water. Beneath one of the ledges an eighteen-inch rainbow materialized to take the fly, and Mike hollered as the hooked trout skimmed over a standing wave. Ten minutes later I caught my own eighteen-inch rainbow around the next bend. The trout was lustrous silver, steely. Like the landscape, it also awaited the vernal brush strokes that would fill in the missing colors.

If your dry fly happens to be a grasshopper and the stream you're on happens to be the Oldman River, the combination can be sublime, as Ian Thomson finds out.

* * *

The Oldman originates high in the Rocky Mountains near the continental divide, where glaciers and snowfields lay like rumpled white quilts among the peaks. Native bull trout, which have inhabited the river's headwaters since the end of the last ice age 10,000 years ago, fin in meltwater pools only a few degrees above freezing. The Oldman quickly swells, however, as it swallows feeder creeks named Oyster, Lyall, Soda, Slacker, and Beehive. As the flow increases, so do the number and variety of fish—cutthroats and rainbows and hybrids of the two.

This upper river is a paradise for someone who likes pocket fishing. Many are the days I've spent flyrodding there for six- to twelve-inch trout, wading upstream past forests of white spruce and trembling aspen. Elk, moose, deer, and bears—both grizzly and black—leave tracks in the sandbars; bighorn sheep and mountain goats scale the vertiginous rock faces overlooking the valley.

As the Oldman courses east toward the foothills and the high plains beyond, the mountains make a final attempt to contain the river at the Livingstone Gap. The gap is a fissure at the edge of the Rockies' front range—a dizzying swirl of water and rock and sky where the constricted river hunches its shoulders and roars. The road signs through the gap caution against *Falling Rock*, but what of *Rising Rock*, so precipitous that claustrophobia is a legitimate concern?

Downstream of the gap the river relaxes, uncoils. The cutthroats begin to thin out as rainbows become predominant. The countryside changes as well, with cattle grazing on vast ridges named Whaleback and Big Coulee. Fields of purple lupine and white daisies bob in the wind. The rutted mud tracks left by ranchers' trucks bisect riverine stands of cottonwood and balsam fir. Some of these stands shelter huge quartzite boulders—pink and white and speckled with russet lichen—deposited by advancing glaciers over 35,000 years ago. This Foothills Erratics Chain extends like a studded tongue from Jasper National Park in west-central Alberta to northern Montana. The largest glacial erratic in North America sprouts from a farmer's field southwest of Okotoks. Thirty-feet high and weighing over 16,000 tons, it's called, appropriately, the Big Rock.

Given the rock's odd location in the nub of agricultural Alberta, it's only fitting that when Calgarian Ed McNally decided to quit law and start a local microbrewery, he called it Big Rock. I should point out that in addition to brewing distinctive beer (I have no stock in the company, though I wish I did), McNally is a keen flyfisher. Two of his products reflect that bias: Royal Coachman Dry Ale, with the classic dry fly printed on the label; and Grasshopper Wheat Ale, a summer thirst-quencher seemingly brewed for bankside consumption on torrid afternoons. The label depicts a giant grasshopper in a field of golden wheat, beside a red grain elevator in a no-name prairie town. The label reminds me so much of the lower Oldman River that I bought a Big Rock "Grasshopper" T-shirt to wear when I fish there.

*   *   *

It was September, and I'd made plans with Ian Thomson to float the tail-water below the Oldman Dam with guide Bob Lowe. I brought the T-shirt, Ian brought the beer, Bob brought the boat and Buddy, the world's greatest fishing dog. The orange three-person raft, in characteristic Bob Lowe fashion, had the word POACHER written in black letters across the pontoons. Bob's a man who doesn't brook conventionality.

The morning was clear but cool. Things warmed up quickly when I caught three nice rainbows in quick succession while Bob readied the raft at the put-in beneath the Cottonwood Bridge. I finally had to vacate when another fly-fisher backed his boat trailer into the middle of the rising fish. We piled into Bob's raft and set off downstream, Buddy doing the canine cha-cha to avoid the maze of fly line, legs, and rod holders scattered across the deck. We hadn't gone 200 yards, however, when Bob oared the raft into shore and told us to hop out. He accompanied Ian to an upstream pool; I ventured downstream with explicit instructions on which run to fish and what tactics to use.

Walking slowly along an exposed bank strewn with fist-sized stones, I cast to at least ten rainbows rising to small mayflies. The fish were evenly spaced along a distinctive drop-off—the water shallow and colorless on one side, deep and blue-green on the other. I caught most of the fish. They ranged in size from ten to fifteen inches and fought wonderfully, veering into the faster current when hooked, the rigid fly line trailing away in a wide arc.

When I rejoined Bob and Ian, it turned out that they had been equally successful. In fact, we stopped and fished from shore so often that it took us over two hours to float the first half-mile of river. The variety of holding water was stupefying, inviting just as many angling techniques. We cast Letort Hoppers along the base of sandstone bluffs, size 18 Blue-winged

Olives over slow-moving weedy slicks, and Royal Trudes among the rippling wavelets beneath gravel fans.

How good was the fishing? Well, sometime about midafternoon, Bob pondered yet another hooked fish, turned to me, and said, "This is ridiculous."

Ian, busy palming his spool while a seventeen-inch rainbow took line, looked at us over his shoulder and replied, "That's the word that sums it up, isn't it?"

Personally, my enthusiasm had waned somewhat when a size 8 hook had become embedded in my little finger, the sharp tip digging into the bone. I'd been fishing two flies—a Royal Trude at the point with a Prince Nymph dropper. The rainbow had taken the Trude, but when I tried to take the fly out of the fish's jaw the trout squirmed free and bolted. When it did, the nymph pierced my pinkie. As if that wasn't painful enough, the embedded fly stuck fast when the sixteen-inch rainbow reached the end of its short tether and began to thrash, tugging my finger this way and that. Finally I managed to corral the runaway fish, but by that time a trickle of blood was dripping off the end of my finger into the river.

That night, back at Bob's place in Beaver Mines, the finger still throbbed as I clinked wine glasses with Ian and Bob to toast one of the best days

Bob Lowe's "Poacher" waits in an Oldman River tailwater.

astream I've ever had. The Australian Shiraz was the same ruby color as the blood I'd donated to the Oldman. We ate two large pizzas—no anchovies—while Buddy curled into a black ball and fell asleep. When the wine was done, we drank the rest of the Grasshopper ale.

"The secret of the whole fishery below that dam is that you've got forty-seven degree water coming out the spout," Bob said. Indeed, during August the water temperature warms as much as ten degrees by the time the Oldman reaches the Summerview Bridge just four miles downstream of the dam. As a result, for the past several years Bob has observed large migrations of rainbows moving upstream into the cooler water, which explains why the late-season fishing is so good.

Predictably, as you move downstream into the Peigan Indian Reserve and beyond, the rainbows thin and the number of brown trout increases. The Alberta government has been stocking browns in the Fort Macleod area, and the couple of times I've flyfished between there and Monarch I've caught a few healthy fourteen-inch browns, indicating that this section could become as noteworthy as the upper river if auspiciously managed. It thrills me to think that one river contains four species of self-sustaining trout: bulls, cutthroats, rainbows, and browns.

Nonetheless, the Oldman has continued to be the focus of the most protracted environmental battle ever waged in Alberta. The controversy surrounding the construction of the Oldman Dam has resulted in native stand-offs, gunfire, abandoned farmsteads, ceaseless debate, and almost a decade of litigation. Built to provide irrigation for downstream farmers, for a time the dam's construction polarized southern Alberta, and you'll still hear the dam discussed in the region's cafes and roadside honkytonks, voices rising and falling like the level of the water behind the 250-foot earthen structure. Much of the debate now takes place in courtrooms, and most of it centers around whether the Alberta government overstepped its bounds when it quashed an environmental group's private prosecution.

Completed in 1991 and costing $450 million, the dam flooded almost thirty miles of the Oldman, Castle, and Crowsnest River watersheds. Friends of the Oldman River (FOR), an anti-dam group, contend the government illegally destroyed fish habitat by constructing the dam, which looms like a stubbed toe on the foot of the Rockies' cordillera, gray and bruised. There's no question fish habitat was destroyed (the dam's construction saddened me, as well), but I think the FOR group is overlooking a crucial point: what about the fish habitat that was *created*? Fact is, the Oldman tailwater has improved the fishery below the dam, and any honest guide or biologist will tell you the same thing.

* * *

The Oldman River derives its name from Na'pi, the great spirit and provider of the Peigan–Blackfoot Indians. Legend has it that Na'pi, after teaching the Peigan to drive buffalo over prairie cliffs, retreated to the river's headwaters and turned himself into a pine tree. From his vantage point atop the continental divide, Na'pi could oversee his Peigan children and the life he had created for them. These days, if Na'pi squints enough and manages to penetrate the dancing, opaque horizon on a blistering summer afternoon, he'll likely see a continuous stream of vehicles arriving at Head-Smashed-In Buffalo Jump, a United Nations' heritage site where the Peigans drove bison over a daunting cliff. During their hunting forays the Indians ceded countless arrowheads to the hardscrabble soil along the Oldman escarpment; some southern Alberta anglers collect them in shoeboxes, a grown-up alternative to marbles.

There are no free-roaming bison anymore, no flying arrows. The only things falling off cliffs are grasshoppers, driven by the wind; the only things waiting to pounce on them are hungry trout. Occasionally, while flyfishing to those trout at the base of a fifty-foot cliff, I get an eerie feeling that a buffalo is about to come tumbling down on me. I glance up but find only blue sky and the planar edge of the bluff. Legends stir uneasily in active imaginations—thoughts are often herded in directions beyond our choosing.

* * *

The drive south to the Oldman River from Calgary is planar as well. Highway 22, a twisting two-lane blacktop, neatly severs the foothills from the prairies, the beef from the grain. The beef is gathered in feedlots, cows milling on piles of brown manure, the stench overpowering. The grain is gathered in elevators, sun-bleached red and green, pigeons swirling around their roofs like flies around a massive head. I can't drive this route without stopping at the Black Diamond Bakery, where the cinnamon knots are fresh and gooey, the perfect accompaniment to a go-cup full of coffee. North of the Oldman River, the highway divides the Whaleback Ridge to the west and the Porcupine

Peigan warriors and buffalo of the past merge with trout and flyfishers of the present on Alberta's Oldman River.

Hills to the east, the latter so-named because their barren slopes are topped by crests of misshapen Douglas fir and limber pine, gnarled by the legendary Chinook winds.

In the fall, usually sometime in mid- to late September, I try to schedule at least one trip to fish the Oldman alone. I prefer that the weather be miserable—overcast and drizzly—because then I'm almost guaranteed good hatches of blue-winged olives. Like most flyfishers, I've always been intrigued by big trout rising to tiny naturals. Last autumn I spent a memorable day on the Oldman catching sixteen-inch rainbows just upstream of the Summerview Bridge. The hatching *Baetis* were sprinkled like pollen across the river, and the large trout gathered in pods to gobble them up.

I wasn't the only one enjoying this spectacle, either. As I walked along the overgrown bank, I startled ghostly great horned owls from their perches, and they swooped across the river and stared back at me with yellow eyes. In an attempt to mitigate the impacts of the Oldman Dam, wildlife biologists have attached huge white birdhouses to a number of cottonwood trunks along this stretch. Judging from the number of owls I spotted that afternoon, their efforts seem to be working. (Also visible from the river are small square openings in some of the sandstone cliffs. Biologists blasted these holes to provide further nesting habitat for falcons and hawks, and the brick masonry used to reinforce the openings is unmistakable.)

The leaf-cluttered game trails had the nutty smell of autumn decay. I pondered, as I always do while following a path trampled by deer, how many ungulate hooves it took to obliterate the narrow swath of vegetation? A game trail is really a ribbon through time. In all likelihood, the same soil I walked upon had been trodden by buffalo and by Peigan warriors in leather moccasins. Bending over, I scraped a finger through the wet earth. I had no way of knowing if Na'pi was watching, but I could see his vaporous breath shrouding the cottonwoods and hear the subtle murmurings of his voice as the Oldman lapped against its banks.

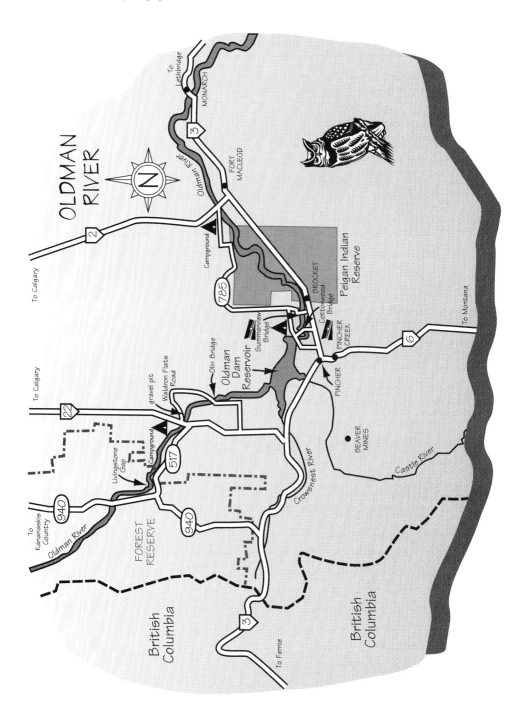

When You Go

Getting There

To reach the upper Oldman River from Calgary, follow Highway 22X west for eleven miles; then turn south on Highway 22 and drive for about eighty-five miles. A highway bridge crosses the river at the Maycroft Campground. Immediately south of the bridge, Secondary Highway 517 follows the Oldman River valley west to the Livingstone Gap and the Rocky Mountains Forest Reserve. To reach the Oldman headwaters, turn north at the junction of Secondary Highway 517 and Highway 940 (Forestry Trunk Road). Drive six miles and then turn west onto the marked logging road paralleling the river.

The fastest route to the Oldman Dam from Calgary is to drive another fifteen miles past the Highway 22 bridge to the junction with Highway 3. Turn east and drive fifteen miles to the junction with Secondary Highway 785. Head three miles north to the dam.

To reach the dam from Montana, take Interstate 15 north to the border. Then follow Highway 4 for seventy miles to the junction with Highway 3 at Lethbridge. Drive west for about sixty-two miles to the junction with Secondary Highway 785. From there continue three miles north to the dam. If you're driving east from British Columbia or north from Kalispell, Montana, an alternate route would be to follow Highway 3 east through the Crowsnest Pass to its junction with Secondary Highway 785 three miles east of Pincher.

River Access

From the river headwaters to just east of the Livingstone Gap, the Oldman flows through a provincial forest reserve and there are no access restrictions. Farther downstream, the next major access point is at the Highway 22 bridge and Maycroft Campground. A mile east of the campground there's another good access point along the Waldron Flats Road, which joins Highway 22 just north of the bridge. Watch for a gravel pit and small road leading down to the river. By continuing along the Waldron Flats Road for another seven miles, eventually you'll come to the trestle Olin Bridge. There's access here as well, but keep in mind that this entire section of the Oldman flows through private ranchland, and you'll have to stay below the high-water mark. (A note of caution: anglers tempted to float the river from Highway 22 to the Olin Bridge shouldn't even think about it—the Maycroft Rapids, a series of ledges and chutes just downstream of the highway, are unnavigable and extremely dangerous.)

The tailwater beneath the dam can be accessed at several spots: Secondary Highway 785 and the day-use site at the dam itself; a mile downstream of the dam via the Cottonwood Road and namesake bridge leading north from Highway 3 about three miles east of its junction with Secondary Highway 785; and at the Summerview Bridge just north of Highway 3 about two miles west of Brocket. Brocket also marks the western boundary of the Peigan Indian Reserve, where trespassers face prosecution. As a result (and since the Oldman flows over a weir on the reserve that can't be avoided without trespassing), the Summerview Bridge is the last practical access point west of Highway 2.

Unfortunately, while the Summerview Bridge provides a convenient take-out for those planning float trips below the dam, at the time of this writing the provincial government has yet to build a public boat ramp immediately beneath the dam, which is certainly called for. If you're using a lighter boat or raft, it's possible to put in at the day-use site, but you'll have to carry the boat several yards to the water. For trailered boats, there's a ramp beneath the Cottonwood Bridge a mile downstream. (Guides on the river also put in elsewhere by private arrangement.) The three-mile stretch of river between the Cottonwood and Summerview bridges is an ideal half- to full-day float, especially if anglers get out and wade the tremendous amount of holding water along the way.

The lower Oldman (downstream of the reserve) can be accessed at Highway 2, Fort Macleod, and the Highway 3 bridge a mile west of Monarch. East of Monarch the current begins to slow and color-up, and the trout thin and give way to warmwater species such as pike, walleye, goldeye, sauger, and sturgeon.

Equipment

The upper Oldman is just the right size for four- and five-weight rods. Because attractor flies work more often than not, you can get away with nine-foot leaders and 4X tippets there. Near its headwaters the Oldman is small enough to ford easily in hip waders, but by the time it reaches the Gap, the volume of water probably warrants chest waders. If you're fishing downstream of the Highway 22 bridge, it might be a good idea to bring along a six- or seven-weight rod as well. The westerlies can howl through this stretch, and the Oldman is a wide, brawling river as it flows beneath the Porcupine Hills and out onto the high plains. It's also worth noting that because several smaller species of mayflies and caddisflies hatch throughout this section, you should definitely have some 5X and 6X tippet material on hand.

Sturdy felt-soled wading boots are a must, particularly downstream of the reservoir. The river bottom there is often coated with slippery yellow and green algae, especially early in the season. By midsummer, run-off has usually scoured the gravelly riverbed enough to provide reliable footing, but the Oldman's current is deceptively swift, and my felt-soled boots give me a sense of surety that I've come to rely on.

In terms of clothing and accessories to bring to the Oldman, put it this way: at the same time it's snowing on Mount Gass where the river rises as a trickle of snowmelt near the continental divide, it might be eighty degrees several hundred miles downstream at Monarch. The best bet is to tote along everything in your flyfishing arsenal, from a fleece jacket to shorts. Come to think of it, that might not be a bad combination.

Fly Patterns

Where to begin? Over the years, I've fished the Oldman with everything from size 4 Woolly Buggers to size 20 Olive Parachutes, from size 6 Bitch Creeks to size 18 Serendipities. They all worked. Rather than repeat myself, see the Fly Patterns listing in the first chapter on the lower Bow River. A similar assortment of dries, nymphs, and streamers will do the trick on the Oldman.

Seasons and Tactics

Below Highway 22 the Oldman is open to fishing all year, though much of the river remains ice-covered until the spring break up. Nevertheless, there's almost always several miles of open water at the tailwater below the dam, and this is a great spot to try on balmy winter days when the urge to fish outweighs the urge to ski. Any fast-sinking nymph or streamer will usually get the attention of at least a few trout. Work the deep pools and make sure your fly is scraping the bottom.

The remainder of the river opens to angling June 1. This date might not mean much if run-off is in full swing, which it generally is. But if for some reason run-off has been delayed—if the snowpack is below average or the spring rains haven't amounted to much—the first couple of weeks the Oldman is open can be exceptional. Most Alberta flyfishers aren't aware that salmonflies hatch in good numbers below the Livingstone Gap, and over the years I've spent a couple of superb days there casting big Sofa Pillows to rising rainbows and cutthroats.

Still, most years run-off is well underway by June and lasts into July. If the lower river is muddy, one option is to try the upper river in the forest reserve, which usually starts clearing a couple of weeks earlier. Expect a good smattering of insects at this time of the year, including golden stones, yellow sallies, green drakes, pale morning duns, caddisflies, and midges. Because the upper Oldman is classic high-mountain pocket water, don't ignore the steeper gradients between the pools and flats. Any lie big enough to hold a fish probably will; watch for current seams around rocks, logs, banks, and eddies. And remember, correctly fishing pocket water has nothing to do with *casting*. Rather, you want to fish a short line to eliminate drag, often doing nothing more than dapping the fly on the surface.

Because the Oldman below the dam isn't a "true" tailwater—that is, some water is also released over the dam during periods of high flow—the river downstream of the reservoir also runs dirty for several weeks in the spring and early summer. However, it's usually clear enough to flyfish by early July, and anglers can expect some great hatches of mayflies, smaller stoneflies, and caddisflies. Even so, my favorite combination along this stretch is an attractor dry fly with a small weighted nymph dropper. (I'm sure you're getting tired of hearing this advice, but what can I say—it works!) Fish the usual spots, paying particular attention to the numerous drop-offs a few feet out from the banks.

Another thing to be aware of below the dam is the river's rate of flow, which will dictate how much wading you can do and whether you'll be able to cross the river at intervals. In Alberta, flow rates are measured in cubic meters per second (cms); for twenty-four-hour information that's updated daily in the summertime, call 403-422-0072. Every angler has his or her own comfort level while wading a swift-moving river, but my experience on the lower Oldman has been that if the flow rate is eighteen cms or less, I can cross the river in relative safety. According to guide Bob Lowe, the ideal discharge for floating is about thirty cms. And remember, during the summer the amount of water being released at the dam has nothing to do with rainfall. To the contrary, since the Oldman Dam was built to provide downstream farmers with irrigation water, often the discharge is highest during the hottest weather.

In southern Alberta, hot and dry weather also marks the height of the grasshopper season. Hopper fishing on the Oldman comes into its own in August and lasts well into the fall. Fish big flies like Letort Hoppers and Stimulators along the banks and below the sandstone cliffs that abut the lower river over much of its length. During September and October, flyfishers should also be on the lookout for blue-winged olives, with the thickest hatches occurring on drab, overcast afternoons.

Special Regulations

Upstream of Highway 22 the Oldman is open from June 1 to October 31. The remainder of the river is open all year. There are some restrictions on certain stretches of the river regarding the number and size of trout that may be kept; see the Alberta regulations for details.

Places to Stay and Eat

There are several provincial campgrounds along the upper Oldman in the forest reserve. It's also possible to park a camper or pitch a tent at numerous primitive campsites along the river. East of the Livingstone Gap, the next major campground is at the Maycroft turnoff at Highway 22. Continuing downstream, you can camp at the Oldman Dam and, beyond that, at the river's junction with Highway 2.

If camping's not your thing, Pincher Creek is only a few miles from the tailwater stretch and has a good selection of motels and restaurants. Contact the Pincher Creek Chamber of Commerce (Box 2287, Pincher Creek, Alta., Canada, T0K 1W0; 403-627-5199).

Guides and Outfitters

Bob Lowe specializes in the area and has been offering float trips below the Oldman Dam longer than anyone. Contact him at Kingfisher Guides' Service

(Box 656, Pincher Creek, Alta., Canada, T0K 1W0; 403-627-5584). Another good bet is Vic Bergman at The Crowsnest Angler (Box 400, Bellevue, Alta., Canada, T0K 1C0; 403-564-4333).

Other Attractions

For Pincher Creek and area, see the "Other Attractions" listing in the chapter on the Castle River. If you're traveling along the lower Oldman, it's worth stopping at Fort Macleod to take in the Fort Museum, a reconstruction of the original fort from which the North-West Mounted Police rebuffed the American whiskey traders in the late 1800s. Constructed on an island along the Oldman River in 1874, Fort Macleod was the first mounted police outpost in Alberta.

7
Elk River

Dave Brown is a short and stocky guide with a barrel chest and thickset arms. When he puts his hands on his hips to watch a client land a fish, he looks a bit like a Mackenzie drift boat tilted on end. Dave's a darn good guide, but his claim to fame occurred several years ago, when fishing author John Gierach immortalized Dave in a magazine column.

Once, while launching a drift boat, Dave managed to run himself over when the emergency brake failed on his truck. Ever the hardheaded guide, he wanted to go ahead with the trip as planned, but the two clients talked Dave into going to the hospital instead. When Gierach fished with Dave a few weeks later, Dave was still limping on a bum knee.

"The only permanent damage," Gierach subsequently wrote, "is that he's now known as Dave 'Speed Bump' Brown." Of course, as a former soldier with the Canadian Airborne Regiment, Dave is no stranger to adversity or, for that matter, leg injuries. During a float trip down British Columbia's Elk River, he told me about a nighttime parachute drop that turned sour. The flight's navigator was supposed to recognize the drop zone by a bright flare on the ground. As it turned out, the over-eager navigator gave the green light when she spotted a dump fire. Rather than float down into a field as planned, the regiment floated down into a forest. Dave broke his ankle when he hung up in a tree. When he described how painful it was for the medics to remove his boot, I could see how getting run over by a truck wouldn't have been such a big deal after all.

We were floating from Sparwood to the Hosmer Bridge—a tight, tricky stretch of the Elk River with lots of log jams and sweepers. It's a stretch I wouldn't tackle without a raft—certainly not in a Mack boat—but Dave has a pair of arms that can stop a drift boat in midstream and make even the roughest water seem stagnant. Despite the fact it was August, a cold front had slipped into the Elk valley, and the air temperature couldn't have been more than a few degrees above freezing. On days like that, vigorous oaring is one of the only ways to stay warm, and I cajoled Dave into letting me paddle through the milder stretches.

"What are we doing out here?" I questioned, my hands turning as blue as my spirits.

"We're after wily westslope cutthroat," Dave replied. The phrase took on the air of an official trip mantra; we began to sing it to the tune of "We're off to see the wizard …" from *The Wizard of Oz*. As any experienced flyfisher can attest, things often get silly in a clammy drift boat on a frigid day.

The rain had turned the river as muddy as our thoughts. To be frank, neither of us had much faith that the trout could see our dry flies through the roily current. Our hunch was confirmed when we floated past a clear-flowing tributary dumping into the Elk.

"Look!" Dave said, pointing to a pod of cutthroats eating big green drake mayflies in the transparent "window" just downstream of the confluence. The mayflies looked like dark leaves turned on edge as they drifted over the waiting trout. Competing for the insects were half a dozen bank swallows; I saw one bird swoop and actually pluck a mayfly from the jaws of a feeding cutthroat. The green drakes were like soldiers caught in a crossfire—they didn't stand a chance. Dave and I clambered out of the boat and rushed to enter the fray, his rod loaded with a four-weight line and H & L Variant, mine with a four-weight line and size 10 Gray Wulff.

We took turns catching fish, methodically working our way up the bank until we realized that stealth really wasn't necessary. The trout were so attuned to the big mayflies that nothing we did distracted them. When we reached the spot where the tributary sluiced down a shale outcropping into the river, Dave took up a position along the downstream seam, and I took the upstream side. Standing about ten feet apart, we hooked fish after fish—chunky westslope cutthroats with amber bellies and spots so black they looked like pinprick holes in the trout's sides. In contrast, the reddish-orange slashes along their lower jaws seemed impossibly bright on that pallid summer day. I brushed a finger along one to see if the radiant color might somehow warm my numb flesh, a gesture akin to holding exposed palms above a campfire.

When we climbed back into the boat, both Dave and I donned every last stitch of available clothing. Synthetic fabric is as popular nowadays as synthetic fly-tying material. In fact, the polar fleece made from recycled plastic pop bottles is almost indistinguishable from Antron dubbing. By the time I'd finished layering underwear, shirts, pullovers, and jackets, I'd begun to resemble an outsized Foam Beetle.

"If the main river was clear, we'd be in cutthroat heaven right now," Dave said as he motioned toward the surface, which was covered in green drakes. It didn't take us long to figure out that the only good dry-fly fishing we were going to have that afternoon was at the Elk's confluence with its tributaries.

"Tribs equal clear water equal fish," Dave muttered. "We're hunting for tribs today."

Sure enough, every time we came across a clear stream entering the Elk, we found rising cutthroats. One of the best things about flyfishing is that you never know what to expect. I suspect Dave felt the same way about being in the airborne regiment, which might explain his easy passage from soldiering to guiding.

*   *   *

Standing around a campfire one night at a barbecue north of Calgary, John Gierach told my wife and I that the Elk River is one of the best wild

Parts of British Columbia's Elk River are tricky, with log jams and sweepers, but Dave Brown has a pair of arms that can stop a drift boat in midstream.

cutthroat streams on the continent. A.K. Best was there as well, and he nodded in agreement. The Elk is often compared to Wyoming's Snake River, and in many ways the comparison is valid. Both are rangy, freestone rivers flowing past idyllic countryside and lofty mountaintops; both have one town that serves as hub and fishing-central for the entire watershed. For the Snake, that town is Jackson; for the Elk, that town is Fernie. However, unlike Jackson, where flyfishing is entrenched and welcomed, many of Fernie's 5,000 residents are having a hard time deciding if the Elk River is a bonanza or a bane. For instance, some local anglers didn't take kindly to a B.C. government decision in 1995 to make the entire Elk watershed catch-and-release. When I asked a grizzled shop owner about the fishing last summer, he waved an arm in the direction of the Elk River and said, "Oh, that's all closed now."

Nevertheless, when you realize what many Elk valley residents have been through over the last decade, it's a bit easier to understand why they're tired of having change thrust down their throats. Fernie, Sparwood, and Elkford all owe their existences to coal mining, but as labor disputes and declining revenue chip away at the industry, many second- and third-generation miners have been forced to choose between destitution and tourism. Look carefully at the callused hands serving cappuccinos at a Fernie coffee shop—a couple of years ago they may have been swinging a pick instead of a spoon.

The clashing ideologies strangely mimic the valley's clashing weather systems. For the most part, the western slope of the Rockies is more temperate than the eastern side, but the melding influences of both Pacific and Arctic air masses nonetheless result in a startling variety of flora and fauna. In fact, the Elk valley forests have the widest assortment of coniferous tree species in the province, including cedar, hemlock, pine, spruce, larch, and juniper. Picture an Oregon forest without the coastal fog, and you begin to get the idea. The wildlife is equally diverse. Along the river be on the lookout for deer, moose, elk, grizzly bears, black bears, cougars, coyotes, beavers, and porcupines.

*   *   *

I was at a Trout Unlimited banquet in Calgary a couple of years ago when I noticed a small crowd gathered around a blown-up photograph on a table top. The photo was part of a display Dave Brown had assembled to auction off a flyfishing trip to southeastern B.C. It showed an angler standing in an aquamarine river, and the photographer had deftly framed the man between the conifers along the bank. All in all, a stunning scene. The group of men stared at the picture and shook their heads.

"No way," said one flyrodder. "I've spent a lot of time down there, and I've never seen water *that* clear. That's not a Canadian river."

"Looks like New Zealand to me," said another. "You're right. It's definitely not in Canada."

Later, when I caught up with Dave, I asked him about the photo. "The Elk?"

"Yeah," he said. "David Lambroughton took it late last summer on a float trip. Not bad, eh?" Lambroughton is a British Columbia-based photographer whose pictures routinely show up in the glossy magazines. His shot of the Elk did indeed remind me of a glassy stream on New Zealand's South Island. Truth is, by August it's not uncommon for the Elk to be that translucent; the chief reason is the river's ample length. Rising beneath ten-thousand-foot peaks along the continental divide, the Elk's headwaters are in fact less than ten miles from Alberta's upper Highwood River, which flows along the same Rocky Mountain trench, albeit on the other side of the continental spine. As the Elk courses southward along the western flank of

Although it's in British Columbia, Albertans such as Kevin Watson have adopted the Elk River and made it one of their own.

the Rockies, the river gradually clears as the glacial till and other waterborne sediment settles along the streambed.

There are trout in the upper river—native westslope cutthroats and bulls—but flyfishing on the Elk doesn't really come into its own until Sparwood, where the current begins to slow and warm, and greater insect populations translate into more and larger fish. How large? Well, my personal best for an Elk River cutthroat is twenty-one inches, but Dave told me Gierach caught one bigger than that when he fished there.

"Where?" I asked, fishing without a rod. Dave just smiled.

* * *

After our fishing trip to the Crowsnest River, described in a previous chapter, Australian guide Will Spry and I decided to head west and spend a few days on the Elk River and its tributaries. Now, Will had spent about a week in Montana's Yellowstone area earlier that month. He'd done a couple of float trips and caught some trout. But nothing, neither in the U.S. nor Down Under, could have prepared him for the time we spent in southeastern B.C.

In a word, Will was flabbergasted. Flabbergasted at the fishing, which never tapered and rewarded us with dozens of cutthroats apiece from daybreak to sunset; flabbergasted at the weather, with afternoon temperatures in the eighties that enabled us to wade wet and still have sweat beading on our foreheads; flabbergasted at the Elk's feeder streams, one of which Will proclaimed the embodiment of everything he'd imagined about flyfishing in the North American Rockies. Granted, he made the comment after releasing a twenty-inch cutthroat with a belly the size of a cement mixer, but I can still see the smile on his face, above the tattered denim shirt and the gold crest of Australia on the bib of his chest waders. Not to mention that he'd spotted a black bear earlier the same day—a thrill tantamount to my first glimpse of an Aussie kangaroo.

That night we camped among the cedars at Mount Fernie Provincial Park. The sparks from our campfire drifted into the sky, merging with the constellations before disappearing and tumbling earthward as black ash. One of those ashes landed on the shoulder of my fleece jacket, melting a hole in the polyester fabric. Years later, every time I slip the jacket on I'm reminded of that trip to the Elk River. I've thought of getting the jacket patched, but decided against it. It would be too much like blindfolding a good eye.

* * *

The day after Dave Brown and I had almost been frozen off the river, we met up with Peter Smallman and his golden retriever, Dame Juliana. Peter is a fly shop owner from Calgary; with his tall, angular frame and silver-tipped beard, he and "Julie" belong in an L.L. Bean catalog. The river had cleared a bit overnight as a warm front blew in from the west, so the three of us (four including Julie) decided to float from the Morrissey Bridge to the Elko take-out. It's a wonderful stretch of the lower river, braided and varied, and we drifted along in the sunshine through spots with names like Cutthroat Corner, The Bank of a Thousand Seams, and The Stink Hole, where Dave and Montana guide Dave Blackburn once smelled a rotting animal.

The Stink Hole is renowned for the size of the bull trout lurking beneath the mottled-brown foam that collects on its surface. A Fernie angler told me he'd landed a ten-pound bull there. As it happens, Peter had been using a streamer most of the day in hopes of hooking a trophy bull, so we lingered at The Stink Hole a while longer than usual. Eventually he caught a foot-long bull, but the big ones weren't moving.

Dave stuck with nymphing and I fished dries—between the three of us, we could have filmed a flyfishing video and had all the bases covered. The choice of technique wasn't a factor anyway. We all caught plenty of trout. Peter even landed a small brookie (they're not common in the Elk but occasionally flush into the river during flooding), giving us three trout species for the day. Several minutes later a seventeen-inch cutthroat rose from behind a rock, silver in the green current, and tried to swallow a size 8 Royal Trude.

"I love the way these fish take a dry fly so delicately," Peter remarked from the back of the boat. "Even in the fast water, it's amazing how *gentle* they can be."

As the afternoon turned to evening and we neared the take-out, all three of us stopped fishing, content to watch the darting birds eat insects in the shards of coppery sunlight, to inhale the resinous odor of the cedars.

In *Just Before Dark*, writer Jim Harrison ruminates about obsessiveness and the sporting life. "We largely do what we do, and are what we are, by excluding those things we find distasteful," he writes. "You reduce your life to those few things that you know are never going to quit."

I have trouble imagining my life without flyfishing. I can't recall exactly when my own emergency brake failed, when flyfishing ran me over and forever altered the person I'd been. Whether or not there is any permanent damage depends on your perception.

Australian guide Will Spry proclaimed one of the Elk's feeder streams to be the embodiment of everything he'd imagined about flyfishing in the North American Rockies.

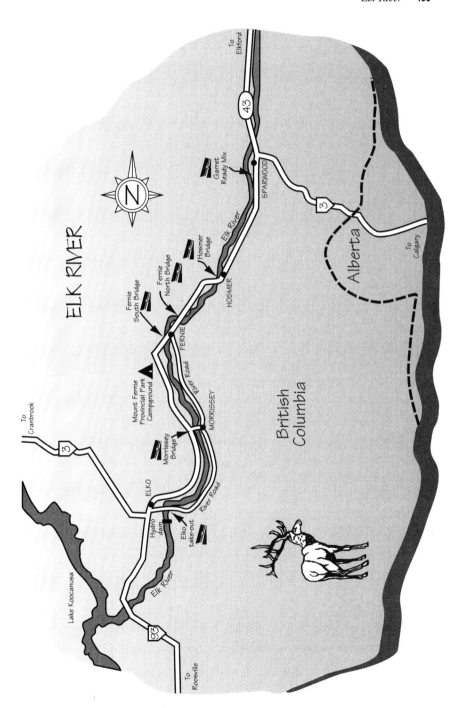

When You Go

Getting There

Located in the extreme southeast corner of British Columbia, the Elk River is easily reached from either Alberta or Montana. From Calgary, take Highway 2 south for about ninety miles; then drive west on Highway 3 for about sixty-five miles to the provincial boundary dividing Alberta and B.C. Continue west on Highway 3 for forty miles to reach Fernie. If you're driving north from Kalispell, Montana, follow Highway 93 north of the Roosville border crossing for about twenty miles and turn east on Highway 3 at Elko. The highway parallels the Elk River valley for the remaining twenty miles to Fernie.

River Access

The Elk, particularly through its lower reaches, is never far from a paved or gravel road. Along its course there are literally dozens of access points, and the put-ins and take-outs have seemingly been designed with the driftboater in mind. The most productive flyfishing starts downstream of Sparwood. A handful of bridges along Highway 3 provide good access, including the Hosmer Bridge, Fernie north and south bridges, and the Morrissey Bridge a half-mile from the Morrissey cut-off. Highway 3 comes close enough to the river in places that you can literally cast from your front bumper. There's also access to the river's east bank upstream of Elko along River Road, reached by crossing the Elk River Reservoir bridge at Elko.

If you're planning a float trip and aren't familiar with the river, I'd suggest any of the following full-day drifts: the Hosmer Bridge to the first (north) bridge at Fernie; the north Fernie bridge to the Morrissey Bridge (this is a long float, so give yourself plenty of time); the Morrissey Bridge to the Elk River Reservoir at Elko. (A warning—you *must* take out at the reservoir bridge, because there's a B.C. hydro dam just downstream. You should also note that the Elk River starts to back up about a mile upstream of the Elko take-out, so anglers choosing this float can expect to do a fair amount of oaring at day's end.)

It's also possible to float from the Garret Ready Mix gravel pit (just south of Sparwood) to the Hosmer Bridge, but I wouldn't recommend this section to anyone who hasn't previously floated it. The rapids, dangerous sweepers, and tight corners can be troublesome for all but the most experienced boaters. Besides, the fishing is just as good, if not better, around Fernie.

Equipment

I prefer a nine-foot, four-weight rod for the Elk, though I've gone lighter on calm days when the cutthroats were rising to small stoneflies or mayflies. Since most of my Elk River fishing is with dry flies, I rarely feel the need to go any heavier than a five-weight, unless the wind's up. A nine-foot leader is all that's required; 4X tippet is plenty small enough, even during a mayfly hatch.

One of the most important things to bring on any Elk River trip are felt-soled wading boots; you might even want to consider metal cleats. The riverbed is treacherously slick—comparable to the Madison River in Montana. It's also a good idea to bring chest waders, because the water's cold and the weather changeable. Nevertheless, the lower Elk valley often gets lengthy heat waves during the summer, so bring along a pair of shorts and be ready to wade wet if it's feasible. When the weather turns nasty, you'll want rain gear and warm clothing, too.

Fly Patterns

I have a running joke with Mike Day, guide and co-owner of Bow River Troutfitters in Calgary. Every time I ask him about the latest cutthroat pattern, Mike just looks at me and laughs: "What *doesn't* work on cutthroats!"

Okay, so maybe he's got a point. That said, my favorite Elk River dry flies are buoyant attractor patterns. Good bets are Lime and Royal Trudes, Royal Wulffs, Madam Xs, Stimulators, and Letort Hoppers in sizes 8 to 14. Smaller mayflies can be imitated with Irresistibles, Borger Yarn Wing Duns, and H & L Variants (sizes 12 to 18). For the big green drakes try Olive or Gray Wulffs in sizes 10 to 14. Don't forget to carry a few Elk Hair and Goddard Caddis (sizes 10 to 18).

I've yet to cast a streamer in the Elk, but I've watched other flyfishers catch cutthroats and bull trout with black, green, and purple Woolly Buggers, sizes 4 to 10. Good nymph patterns include Brooks' Golden Stone, Montana, and Bitch Creeks nymphs in sizes 4 to 10, as well as Gold-ribbed Hare's Ear (sizes 8 to 18) and Beadhead Prince (sizes 10 to 16).

Seasons and Tactics

Most of the lower Elk freezes during the winter, but I've never wanted to fish it then anyway. As I've said, to me cutthroat trout are synonymous with dry flies, and for that reason I rarely flyfish the Elk prior to July. Sometimes I have no choice. The Elk drains mountainous country renowned for its huge snowpack, and the river often remains unfishably muddy until the second week of July. The good news is that by the time it does clear, the hatches are in full swing.

"I've seen golden stones come off this river as thick as caddisflies," said guide Dave Brown. When they do, you're apt to be in for some of the most thrilling dry-fly fishing of your life. There's nothing subtle about the way the trout slash at the big stonefly naturals. And there's nothing subtle about how to imitate them, either. Tie on a big yellow-bodied Stimulator or Letort Hopper; giving the fly a little motion often rouses the fish even more. Basically, cast wherever you see trout working. If I know golden stones have been hatching but there are no naturals on the water, I'll nymph along the river bottom with a Brooks' Golden Stone or similar imitation. Because of the Elk's cold water and relatively high elevation, the golden stones are usually around most of the summer. Peak hatches are in July and early August. Most of the egg-laying activity—and thus the best dry-fly fishing—occurs in the afternoon and evening.

Stonefly adults are most active on sunny or slightly overcast days. When it's cloudy and rainy, the pre-eminent Elk River hatch is green drakes. The hatch usually begins in the afternoon and lasts into the evening. Watch for them to emerge throughout the river. I've seen good hatches of green drakes on the Elk until the end of August and even into the fall.

The green drakes and golden stones are the Elk River hatches I anticipate most, but you'll also see good numbers of smaller stoneflies, pale morning duns, and caddisflies. Not that it really matters, however, because matching the hatch is a formality that can easily be forsaken by Elk River flyrodders. Even on days when no fish are rising, I generally manage to catch plenty of cutthroats by prospecting with an attractor dry fly in good holding water. Concentrate on pockets, bankside and underwater structure, eddy lines, and the tails of gravel riffles. Anglers should note that only one hook at a time is allowed on the Elk and its tributaries.

The Elk fishes well until early October, but once the yellow leaves start collecting on the river bottom, the cutthroats seem to lose interest. In turn, so do I.

Special Regulations

The Elk River is closed from April 1 to June 15 to allow the cutthroat trout to spawn in peace. During the open season, fishing is catch-and-release only throughout the river and its tributaries. (This is a newly-instituted regulation that may change in the future. Check the current B.C. Freshwater Fishing Regulations for up-to-date information.)

Also note that you'll need a B.C. freshwater license to fish in the province. These are available at several sporting goods shops and gas stations at Fernie and Sparwood. You can also purchase a B.C. license in Alberta at The Crowsnest Angler along Highway 3 (22614 27th Ave., Bellevue; 403-564-4333). B.C. licenses cost about $30 (American) per year for U.S. anglers; eight-day licenses ($19) and one-day licenses ($7.50) are also available.

Places to Stay and Eat

The Elk River valley is filled with first-rate accommodations. For general information, contact Fernie Central Reservations (31 Timberline, W. Fernie, B.C., Canada, V0B 1M1; 250-423-9284). Note that the area code for all B.C. listings changed to 250 from 604 in October 1996.

If you're traveling in a group, I personally recommend the Timberline Village Condominiums at the ski hill (52 Timberline Cres., Box 1316, Fernie, B.C., V0B 1M0; 800-667-9911). Fernie also has some great bed-and-breakfasts. My favorite is the Elk River Chalet, situated on the river's west bank six miles south of Fernie along Highway 3. From the solarium, you can see whether trout are rising as you eat breakfast or dinner (9465 Highway 3, W. Fernie, B.C., Canada, V0B 1M0; 250-423-7769).

If you're camping, try Mount Fernie Provincial Park just southwest of Fernie off Highway 3. It's got great sites surrounded by towering cedars; the smell alone is worth the stay. If the park campground is full, head for the Snowy Peaks RV Park at Hosmer or the West Crow RV Park at Elko.

Fernie has several good restaurants—none as good as Rip & Richard's Eatery right beside the south Fernie bridge on Highway 3. The big outdoor deck overlooks the Elk River, and the food, beer, and service are exceptional.

Guides and Outfitters

The Elk River guiding industry is undergoing a shake-out of sorts as resident anglers realize you can't just hang a sign outside your door and call yourself a guide. As a result, it wouldn't be fair of me to recommend anyone I haven't fished with. Contact the Fernie Chamber of Commerce (Highway 3 and Dicken Road, Fernie, B.C., Canada, V0B 1M0; 250-423-6868) and tell them *exactly* what you expect of a guide and an Elk River float trip.

Someone I *have* fished with and highly recommend is Calgary guide Dave Brown at the Elk River Angler (403-285-1668, phone and fax). Dave specializes in the Bow and Elk Rivers and arranges for transportation between Calgary and Fernie. Another good source of Elk River information is Vic Bergman at The Crowsnest Angler (22614 27th Ave., Bellevue; 403-564-4333).

Other Attractions

The Elk River valley is an outdoor enthusiast's dream. Mountain biking, hiking, rafting, horseback riding, nature photography, and birdwatching—those are just a sampling of what's available. Fernie still has the feel of a turn-of-the-century town—a tour of the brick and stone heritage buildings, built after a huge fire virtually destroyed Fernie in 1908, should rank high on any itinerary. The Royal Hotel, constructed in 1909 and located at 501 1st Avenue, is a great place to grab a beer and shoot a game of pool. Also worth a visit is The Arts Station, 601 1st Avenue, built in 1908 for the Canadian Pacific Railway. Among its attractions are a ninety-seat theater, pottery studio, photography lab, and other studios where artists paint, work on stained glass, quilt, spin, and weave. The station's Whistle Stop restaurant serves light lunches and great homemade soup.

Part Three

North of Calgary

8
North Raven River
(Stauffer Creek)

A spring creek, by nature, emerges from the subterranean world imbued with mysticism. Whereas most streams begin as a trickle of water at the foot of a glacier or as a coalescence of run-off from a mountain valley, a spring creek is different. One moment it's not there and the next moment it is, the hydraulic equivalent of a magician pulling a rabbit from a hat.

I've never seen a rabbit along the banks of central Alberta's North Raven River, but I have seen a mouse. It ran across the water. It didn't swim. It didn't walk. It ran. It didn't appear to get even its belly wet, and I wondered what Isaac Newton would have made of it, or anyone else obsessed by physics. In retrospect, I'm sure it had something to do with surface tension and tiny feet. Yet since it happened on a spring creek, I'm not prepared to rule out mysticism, either.

More important is that just upstream of where that mouse crossed the creek, I sat on a clump of green grass and watched three or four brown trout feeding in a pool. The sun had set minutes before, directly in my line of sight, and the browns were sipping small caddisflies from the mauve-colored surface. Sipping is the only way to describe it. The rises were so imperceptible, so measured, that I would have written them off to mysticism as well, except that I'd fished the stream often and knew better. I also knew that the browns were large, because small trout don't rise that way, especially after sunset in a pool where size is boss. I scrutinized the nearest riseform until I figured that I had the trout's feeding pattern down pat. Every ten seconds another dimple. Clockwork.

I held my right arm high above my head to avoid tangling the loose line in the grass, and cast. An awkward motion, bereft of grace, but effective. The fly landed about twelve feet ahead of me, and I stripped in line as it swirled on the spiraling current. The trout rose. I struck … missed. Dammit! I waited another ten seconds—another five minutes—but the trout didn't resume feeding. Neither did the other trout that had been rising in the pool. The North Raven is like that—often you only get one chance. I'd had my chance and blown it; I decided to walk back to the truck.

A farm tractor droned in the distance. Mosquitoes droned in my ears. Other than that I heard only the gurgle of the stream when I paused along its overgrown banks. When American naturalist David Quammen described a spring creek as "a thing of sublime and succoring constancy," he must have been listening to the same sound. That gurgle never lets me down, even when the brown trout do. It's there in the winter and it's there in the summer. It lulls me to sleep at night. It washes away the grime of civilization. Record companies have placed their microphones beside a stream and marketed that gurgle, but such attempts inevitably fall short because they evoke no recollection on the part of the listener. Without recall the gurgle is soothing but insignificant, a noise out of place and time. I thought of the North Raven's gurgle, once more, as I drove away on the gravel road. The evening had been fishless; the gurgle sustained me.

*   *   *

The legal name is the North Raven River, though how anyone could name a creek that size a "river" is beyond me, since it's rarely more than a dozen feet across. Many locals refer to it as Stauffer Creek, named after a tiny village along nearby Secondary Highway 761. The village doesn't have much to offer the visiting angler; the most noteworthy building is a waste processing facility. There's a post office and a general store, and there are usually a few American kestrels perched on the roadside telephone wires, easily identified by their blue wings and ocher backs and tails. From their lofty perches they oversee a checkered countryside of open pasture interspersed with groves of aspen and spruce. The diversity of species, both plant and animal, is amazing. It results from the meeting of two distinct natural regions—boreal forest and aspen parkland. In turn, Stauffer Creek sustains its own riverine habitat as it weaves its way through meadows, swamps, and inscrutable thickets of willow and alder.

As the crow flies (or the kestrel, or the yellow warbler, or the cedar waxwing, or any of the dozens of bird species that live here), Stauffer Creek has about five miles of fishable water. But if that crow were to fly a foot or two above the surface, were to follow every convoluted bend and loop and fly past every beaver dam, the distance would probably be ten times that much, maybe twenty. You can walk for hours along Stauffer Creek, struggling through the willows and fishing the runs and pools, and then exit the streamside brush to find that you're staring at the same herd of cows you were when you began. Speaking of cattle, once I rolled under the bottom strand of a barbed-wire fence, stood up, and realized I was ten yards from a solitary bull, its scrotum dangling. Although I stuck to the fence line and backed away, he snorted and bellowed, mucous dangling from a flared black nostril. Stauffer Creek is not without its hazards.

It was June, the banks were blotched with yellow marsh marigolds, and love was in the air. So were the green and brown drake mayflies, the North Raven's pre-eminent early-season hatches. These mayflies are impressive insects. Both have three tails; both are large and showy. Their hatches often overlap, the green drakes coming off during the afternoon and evening, the brown drakes after twilight and well into the night. The first time I saw a brown drake in flight I couldn't believe my eyes. The dun was an inch high, the mahogany-colored veins in its mottled wings as apparent as a poplar leaf's. It stalled in flight, by turns gaining and losing altitude, and reminded me of the balsa-wood planes I used to throw across the yard as a kid.

I've seen trout rising to brown drake duns and spinners along the North Raven, but I've yet to really hit the hatch at its peak. It only lasts for three or four nights, usually sometime during the first two weeks in June, and I don't have the luxury of being on the stream every night as some of the locals do. For me it's strictly a hit-and-miss affair, the misses far outnumbering the hits.

The green drakes are more reliable. Slightly smaller than the brown drakes but still huge by Alberta mayfly standards, the western green drake hatches best on blustery, drizzly days, also during the first two weeks in June. Watch for them along the stream's faster gravel-bottomed sections. Actually, it's impossible to miss the green drakes during a heavy emergence. Their lime bodies and bluish wings look like puffs of smoke dancing along the surface; their outsized eyes, the color of red wine, are unmistakable. This is one of the few North Raven hatches that will pull the trophy browns out of their lies and into the middle of the stream to feed, and it's quite a sight to see a half-dozen twenty-inch browns jockeying for position like horses along a backstretch.

The North Raven River is one of those streams where you only get one chance. Miss that chance and you might just as well be on your way.

*   *   *

I prefer to fish the North Raven by myself. A stream this intimate invites solitude, and the voice of another angler—even the swish of another fly line—taints the experience. Fishing alone isn't without certain perils, however. You could easily twist an ankle in one of the beaver furrows that radiate from the stream, and your pleas for help could easily be mistaken for a sick cow by the flyfishers back at the parking lot. The swamp, situated about midway between the Stauffer and Buck for Wildlife bridges, isn't a place to be after dark. I even try to avoid it during the *daytime*, what with its oozing muck and bottomless possibilities. You could walk too far on a hot day, become dehydrated, and risk collapsing in the willows. That happened to me once. And I'd hate to get caught in the middle of an open field when one of the frequent summer thunderstorms rolls in off the eastern slope of the Rockies, the clouds silver with white trim from a distance, then gray, then charcoal as the first raindrops spat on the water. Lightning bolts have an affinity for graphite, and a flyfisher in this predicament is as vulnerable as a golfer holding the pin.

Yet I still prefer to fish alone, climbing into and out of the creek as I make my way upstream, crossing back and forth from side to side as dictated by the riparian vegetation and whimsy. Upstream of the Lazy M guest ranch, west of Stauffer, the North Raven holds brook trout as well as browns. Both are lovely and wild. Although the fish are smaller here on average, this is my favorite section.

When I fished it last September, the creek drew me on, upstream, and before long I was back in the truck with a topographic map spread across the passenger seat, trying to locate the spring's source. With the map and some persistence, I finally found it down the road from the faded yellow Butte Community Hall, and though the landowner eyed me suspiciously when I told him I just wanted to look at the spring, he relented and showed me the way.

I'm not sure what I expected. A geyser, maybe, bursting from the ground like Old Faithful. Or at least a cavern with water pouring out of the darkness. But the spring, located at the bottom of a hill beneath a red barn and a white fence, didn't gush; the only evidence that it came out of the ground at all was a slight upwelling just beyond a pair of red-winged blackbirds sitting on the marsh grass. I listened closely. There was a slight fizz, the sound a soda makes if you put your ear to the can. When I walked back to the truck along an overgrown path, passing beneath a shady arch of balsam poplar, the landowner came up the drive with the day's mail clenched in one hand.

"Did you see it?" he asked.

"Yeah. Thanks for letting me take a look. I fish this stream a lot, and I've always been sort of curious to see where it begins."

He told me the spring is actually an aquifer from the Clearwater River, about two miles away. I thought of all that water rushing underground, sweeping past fossils and bones, and the mysticism returned. Then and there I vowed that I'd never fish a spring creek again without attempting to locate the source.

*   *   *

Coincidence or not, one of the best areas to flyfish the North Raven is between the Buck for Wildlife and Stauffer bridges, generally known as the "Buck for Wildlife" section. (Alberta's Buck for Wildlife program provides funds for habitat improvement and public access to wildlife areas.) The average brown trout is larger here than elsewhere in the stream, and over the years several organizations, including the Alberta Fish and Game Association and the Central Alberta chapter of Trout Unlimited, have worked wonders to improve the quality of the fishery. Cooperative landowners along the stream have permitted the installation of almost nine miles of barbed-wire fencing, keeping the livestock at bay and cutting down on bank erosion. Unfortunately, the beavers have been harder to contain. Each year dams are dynamited and the stream's flow restored; each year the beavers build anew, Canada's mammalian equivalent of the U.S. Army Corps of Engineers. I know of one central Alberta angler who flyfishes with a shotgun slung across his back, and while he releases all the trout he catches, the beavers aren't as fortunate.

I've had my own run-ins with beavers, though I've yet to shoot one. Sometimes, usually just as I'm preparing to cast to a twenty-inch brown, a beaver will plop into the stream and start swimming my way. My first impulse is to wave my arms in the air and shout, but all that does is cause the beaver to slap its tail on the water in alarm, and fish don't like slaps on the water. The best approach is to huddle against the bank and hope the beaver swims past without spotting you. North Raven trout are used to beavers and usually resume rising within minutes of one passing by. That's exactly what happened to me one August evening a few summers ago. Able to conceal myself by kneeling in the bankside grass, I watched a beaver swim through the pool I was scouting, round the bend, and disappear. A trout rose. Then another. And another.

The humidity that evening was stifling. My glasses kept sliding down my nose, eventually fogging so badly that I had to take them off and slip them into a vest pocket. Sweat beaded on my forehead; condensation beaded on the grass. The intensity rose. The sun set. I had a sensation of fumbling on the jungle floor for a lost set of keys. A frog slipped into the water as I slipped a 6X tippet through the eye of a size 20 Elk Hair Caddis. A cast wasn't necessary. All I did was part the grass and dangle the fly on the pool, slowly rotating my arm clockwise to ensure the fly drifted naturally and didn't drag. Sure enough, an amber streak materialized in the dusky water and took the artificial. The brown trout, about eighteen inches, chose to fight vertically, sounding to the bottom of the pool until pressure and persistence did it in. If the fish had run horizontally, either upstream or down, thick surface weedbeds likely would have changed the outcome. Don't believe anyone who tells you that flyfishing is all skill and no luck.

The North Raven River is a stream so intimate that it invites solitude, and the voice of another angler taints the experience.

* * *

A man and a mouse—those are the two strangest things I've ever seen along the North Raven. You've already heard about the mouse. Let me tell you about the man. He was parked at the Buck for Wildlife bridge, and I hadn't been talking to him for more than five minutes when he rummaged in the back seat of his car and produced an envelope. Inside were black-and-white aerial maps. He laid them carefully across the tailgate of my truck until, from end-to-end, they formed a stream.

"Stauffer Creek!" exclaimed the Map Man. "In its entirety." I wondered about *his* entirety—specifically, what was missing. He then pulled out a three-dimensional binocular apparatus, boasting that it cost $100 and had military origins. He insisted that I have a look through it at the maps. Sure enough, there it was—the North Raven from ten-thousand feet. It wound through farmers' fields and groves of trees. It flowed under bridges, including the one thirty feet from where we stood.

"Pretty neat, eh?" said the Map Man, staring at me with the expectant twitch of a dog waiting for a scratch behind the ears.

"Yes," I replied. "Not bad." That's all I could come up with. I didn't know what else to say. The Map Man carefully placed the stream back in the manila envelope, but before I could finish rigging up and bid him *adieu*, he unveiled more photos of other provincial streams and rivers—again, all viewed from the cockpit. I discovered that the Map Man was a Boy Scout leader, which explained a lot. Although they're generally well-intentioned and there's no denying the good they do, most of the Scout leaders I've met tend to obfuscate the simplest pursuits.

I wondered what Isaac Newton would have made of the Map Man. I wondered if the Map Man had ever been hit on the head by a falling apple or a size 2 Zonker. I wondered, finally, if he'd ever seen a mouse run across the water.

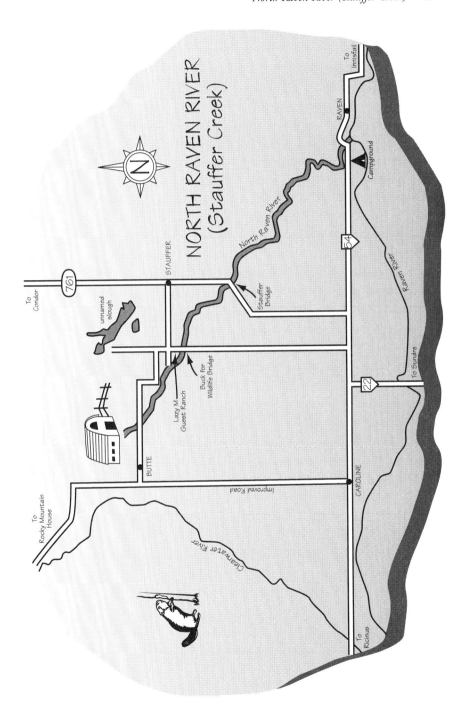

When You Go

Getting There

From Calgary, follow Highway 2 about seventy miles north to Innisfail. Then take Highway 54 west; after about twenty miles you'll come to a bridge across the North Raven. Don't bother trying to fish the stream here. Instead, continue for another five miles along Highway 54 and take the northbound turnoff for Stauffer at Secondary Highway 761. Drive four miles to the Stauffer bridge. There's parking beside the bridge and good fishing upstream.

River Access

Almost all the land along the North Raven is private, and many of the landowners are choosy about whom they'll let on. Fortunately, as I mentioned, the Buck for Wildlife section between the Stauffer and Buck for Wildlife bridges provides miles of great public fishing. Fencing keeps the livestock out, and several ranchers have installed stiles over the barbed-wire fences, reducing the chance of snagging your waders and ruining your day before it begins.

To reach the Buck for Wildlife bridge, continue along Secondary Highway 761 until you reach Stauffer, about two miles north of the Stauffer bridge. Turn left and head west for two miles along an improved gravel road. Then turn left and travel south for half a mile to the bridge. There's a parking lot just across the bridge on the left-hand side—watch for the two outhouses and the large Buck for Wildlife sign. There's great flyfishing both upstream and down.

There's yet another bridge and access point about a mile upstream of the Buck for Wildlife bridge. To reach it, stay on the improved gravel road heading west from Stauffer until the road crosses the creek just before a deadend. There's good brown trout fishing downstream as the North Raven winds past the Lazy M guest ranch. Upstream the fish tend to be smaller, with brook trout present in good numbers as well.

Equipment

Of all the rivers and streams in this book, this is the one where you want to bring your three- and four-weight rods. Resist the temptation to go any lighter; you'll need some backbone in case you hook one of the five- or six-pound browns that lurk in the deepest pools. I prefer a shorter rod here—something in the seven- to eight-and-a-half-foot range. Not only will it be easier to carry along the willowy banks, but you'll want a rod that can throw short, tight loops to avoid hanging up on your backcasts.

Tippet material should range from 3X (for streamers and bigger nymphs) to 6X (for small dries). Odds are you won't land that big brown hooked on a tippet that fine, but at least you won't send it fleeing for cover while casting. Use nine- to twelve-foot leaders in the tight spots, even longer leaders if space permits.

Depending on the weather and time of year, I may fish the North Raven in chest waders or in hip waders or wade wet. Use common sense. If it's August, sunny, and eighty degrees, neoprene chest waders could be fatal. (Don't laugh. I've seen heat-exhausted flyrodders, their hats soaked in sweat, trudging along the North Raven in chest waders on some of the hottest days of the year.) If possible, I like to wade wet. It's easier to walk through the brush without waders on, and much of the stream is too deep for hip waders, particularly if you take into account the bothersome silt and mud along some stretches.

As for clothing, take along the usual assortment of three-season Alberta apparel. Though the North Raven is quite far from the mountains, this area of the province is notorious for late-afternoon and evening thunderstorms that sweep east over the foothills and onto the grasslands. Even during the hottest weather, I pack rain gear if I'm planning to walk any distance from the truck.

Fly Patterns

Upstream of the Lazy M guest ranch, where the trout tend to be smaller and brookies are just as common as browns, try using size 14 or 16 attractor dry flies—things like Royal Wulffs, Yellow Humpies, and Royal and Lime Trudes. This is the one section of the North Raven where fishing dry flies blind occasionally pays off. As you travel farther downstream, browns predominate, growing larger and more selective. To imitate the hatches of smaller mayflies, including blue-winged olives and PMDs, I use the usual array of Adams, Irresistibles, and Borger Yarn Wing Duns, sizes 14 to 18. When the big brown drakes or green drakes start coming off, try a size 10 or 12 Gray or Olive Wulff. Your dry fly box should also include a few Elk Hair and Goddard Caddis (sizes

10 to 18), Stimulators and Letort Hoppers (sizes 8 to 12), and black beetle patterns such as Jack Dennis' deer-hair version in sizes 12 to 16.

For nymphing, I rarely use anything but Pheasant Tails and Gold-ribbed Hare's Ears, maybe sliding a brass bead over the tippet if I'm looking for extra weight. (This is a great technique, first shown to me by guide Bob Lowe. By slipping the bead over the tippet before you tie the fly on, you get the same effect as incorporating a bead into the fly. The difference is that you can remove the bead whenever you want, essentially giving you two flies in one.)

Streamers work well on the North Raven through the spring and early summer, but they're not much use as the season progresses and weed growth thickens. My favorite patterns are small black Woolly Buggers and Zonkers, sizes 8 and 10. Anglers planning to fish the stream in September should also come equipped with water boatmen imitations (sizes 10 to 16). Although I've never seen it, the browns reportedly go crazy for these odd insects at this time of year.

Seasons and Tactics

Some diehards fish the North Raven year-round. I usually make my first trip there in late March or early April. This is the time of year to cast weighted streamers into deep pools, letting the fly sink before starting a quick, jerky retrieve. Another good bet is to work the streamer along sunken logs or other underwater structure. Warm spring days also bring the promise of dry-fly fishing, and nothing gets rid of my winter blues faster than a pod of Stauffer Creek browns rising to blue-winged olives before Easter.

Spring and early summer are also good times to nymph. My favorite method is to tie a small Pheasant Tail or Hare's Ear on a foot-long dropper beneath an attractor dry fly—maybe a Royal Wulff or Lime Trude. The dry fly acts as an indicator, and every now and then a trout will surprise you and pluck it from the surface. Another favorite technique of mine, picked up during a trip to New Zealand a few years back, is to affix a small piece of fluorescent yarn to the leader with a slip knot and use that as an indicator. Adjust the distance between the yarn and the weighted nymph according to how deep the trout are feeding. This is especially effective when you can see the fish feeding beneath the surface.

By June I'm usually fishing nothing but dries on the North Raven. Watch for the green and brown drakes to start hatching, if you're lucky enough to be on the river during the first and second weeks of the month. Both emergences can be sporadic, but if you hit them right, you'll never forget the experience. Green drakes hatch best in blustery weather during late afternoon and evening, brown drakes just before dark and at night. Other reliable hatches during June and July are the pale morning duns and several varieties of caddisflies. But remember, tying on the right fly is just the start—North Raven browns are extremely wary. To be successful, expect to spend a lot of time on your knees.

As the hatches begin tapering off in late July and into August, the trout tend to become more active in the evenings. Look for them in the corner pools and along heavily undercut banks unaffected by weed growth, which becomes troublesome as the summer progresses. If you do fish during the day, try casting a black beetle or grasshopper pattern to the holding water along the banks, giving the line an occasional short strip to imitate a struggling terrestrial. As autumn rolls around and the days get cooler, the blue-wings once again provide the bulk of the dry-fly fishing. Keep an eye out for them during midafternoon on overcast days. When blue-winged olives are not in evidence, I spend most of my time nymphing to sighted fish at this time of the year. Don't forget to watch for those water boatmen.

Special Regulations

There are no special regulations concerning flyfishing on the North Raven.

Places to Stay and Eat

The Lazy M guest ranch is a great place to stay *and* eat. Whether you stay in the lodge or in the original log cabin, the ranch fronts some of the best flyfishing water on the creek. A ten-minute drive will bring you to other good nearby streams and rivers, including Prairie Creek, South Raven River, Clear Creek, and the Clearwater River. Book ahead (Box 427, Caroline, Alta., Canada, T0M 0M0; 403-722-3053). The nearest motel accommodation is at Caroline. To get there, take Secondary Highway 761 south of Stauffer to Highway 54. Then travel west for five miles to the town. Try the Caroline Motel (Box 400, Caroline, Alta., Canada, T0M 0M0; 403-722-3000). There are a couple of decent restaurants and bars along the highway, but don't expect much. I asked for a microbrew beer in a tavern once, and the waitress gave me a queer look.

"I think we had that once," she said, "but not now. Can I get you a Bud?" For those preferring to camp, the Raven River Campground is ten miles east of Caroline along Highway 54.

Guides and Outfitters

A few Calgary guides will range this far if you ask them, but I'd recommend Ron Manz from Rocky Mountain House. He specializes in central Alberta, and seems to be on a first-name basis with several of the North Raven browns. Reach Ron at Before the Hatch Anglers (Box 2304, Rocky Mountain House, Alta., Canada, T0M 1T0; 403-845-4435) or through Ram River Sports (403-845-4160).

Other Attractions

The Lazy M guest ranch offers excellent horseback riding across miles of rolling pastures and through birch, spruce, and pine woods. If you're a birder, bring along your binoculars and prepare to marvel at the number of species inhabiting the overlapping parkland and deciduous and coniferous forests. If you've got the time, Rocky Mountain House, about twenty-five miles north-west of Caroline, is worth visiting. Make sure to take in the Rocky Mountain House National Historic Site, which features the remains of four centuries-old trading forts, a burial ground, and archaeological exhibits. The visitor's center also recounts the area's fur-trading history and includes exhibits of western-Canadian Indian artifacts.

9
Prairie Creek

Dawn at Prairie Creek. The pink light flowed over the treetops, collected on the water's surface, crawled up my arms. Pink mingled with fuchsia mingled with topaz, and the pastels enveloped me, caressed me, seduced me. An object in the stream caught my attention. A silver beer can with blue flanks, rolling over and over in the current like a played-out fish. I reached for my net and thrust it in the creek, snaring the metallic impostor. *Wildcat,* read the lettering. But the can had been opened, the cat gutted. Empty or not, it was still the first catch of the day.

A red squirrel ran out on a fallen spruce trunk and stopped instantly when it saw me. It chattered a noisy alarm, its russet body vibrating. A squirrel with an attitude. Relenting, I left the pool to the squirrel and moved on. As the sun flickered through the woods, shadow and light jockeyed for position on the water, melding and parting, warming and cooling. The current pushed steadily against my ankles, the gravel shifted uneasily beneath my feet. Even the smallest stream has a way of making you feel like an intruder, and the idyllic notion of becoming one with nature is quickly dashed when you realize that nature wants nothing to do with you. A territorial squirrel would tear your head off if it thought it stood a chance.

I stripped some line from the reel and started casting over a dark pool flecked with white bubbles. As the first loop formed, droplets of water sprayed from the line, glinting and then dissolving in a shower of iridescent sparkles. I could have put the fly down, but I chose to keep false casting, spellbound by the whistling line and the precise curve it traced through the air. I finally dropped my wrist and tumbled the streamer into the head of the pool. I retrieved line as fast as necessary to keep the leader taut, flicking the rod tip as the purple Woolly Bugger skimmed the cobbles along the bottom.

When most of the line lay coiled at my feet, the leader hesitated in the water directly in front of me, and I struck. A foot-long brook trout surged to the top of the pool, showing me its vermiculated back and orange pectoral fins before diving again. It fought well but quickly came to hand, no match for twentieth-century graphite.

When asked about Prairie Creek, Alberta fisheries' biologist Kerry Brewin told me it has the highest number of brook trout of any stream he'd ever sampled. I thought of that as I fished the center fork just inside the forest reserve. Before long the bird calls and sounds of the creek were augmented by the rumble of logging trucks on the nearby highway. "The funeral procession for the forests," a man once told me. The eighteen-wheel hearses were empty as they headed west into the foothills; they'd be loaded with corpses on the return trip later in the day. The banks along upper Prairie Creek are also a coniferous graveyard of sorts, the deadfall and log jams providing ideal cover for trout.

As the morning progressed and sunlight struck more of the water, I switched to a bright streamer—a size 6 Woolly Bugger variant with a white ostrich-herl tail and gold-ribbed burgundy chenille body. It worked wonders on the brown trout—they darted out from the submerged timber to smash the garish pattern. The trick was to cast the fly about eight inches from the edge of a sunken log or root ball, then let the current sweep the streamer downstream like an aqueous comet, its ivory tail streaking through the water. The casts had to be perfect. If the fly landed too far from the logs, the browns would ignore it, too close and I'd be tight to a week's supply of firewood.

Atop the embankment a forestry worker came out of a small cabin in the pines. He saw me and stopped to watch, waving when he caught my eye. I continued up the creek and caught a few more browns, their gold sides flashing in the sunlight as they chased the streamer. Even when the fly seemed to be moving too fast to be caught—seemed to be sweeping downstream twice as fast as the current—the trout never missed. Unfortunately, I couldn't make the same claim. For every brown hooked, I missed another, pulling the streamer out of its mouth or striking too late. The biggest fish landed was fourteen inches, but I lost another that might have gone eighteen, a black-spotted brute that beelined for the deadfall and tied an underwater macramé knot with my leader.

*   *   *

I try to avoid littering streams with anthropomorphic rubble, but if I had to come up with one word to describe Prairie Creek it would be this: quirky. Even during the lowest flows late in the season, the water is never colorless.

It's either tannic or olive or some other combination of yellow-green-brown, but it's never perfectly clear. I don't know why, exactly, though I suspect it has something to do with the groundwater leaching into the streambed, and all that logging activity near the creek's headwaters. Prairie Creek is very sensitive to rainfall. It muddies quickly and tends to stay that way long after other streams in the area have cleared (yet another result of logging and soil erosion). That said, it's a good idea to monitor the central Alberta weather before planning a trip to Prairie Creek. If you're already at the creek when it blows out, head southeast to the nearby North Raven River, which is actually a spring creek and is rarely unfishable.

Other options are provided by the handful of lakes around Prairie Creek—some of the best stillwater fishing spots in Alberta. Strubel Lake has rainbows to five pounds; I like to fish along its reedy shorelines from a kick boat or float tube. Mitchell Lake, less than a mile north of Strubel, has some big brook trout in addition to rainbows. Cow Lake is large, shallow, and located about midway between Rocky Mountain House and Strachan. It's susceptible to winter kill, but when the trout survive, Cow ranks among the province's best lakes, with rainbows to twelve pounds.

The brown trout grow just as big at Swan Lake to the southwest. The Alberta record brown was caught there in 1991, a thirty-four-inch fish that weighed seventeen-and-a-half pounds. Swan also has brookies, lake trout, and northern pike to about fifteen pounds, though larger ones are caught occasionally. All in all, a real mixed bag.

How quirky is Prairie Creek? Well, consider that its north fork is largely a series of sloughs, home to marsh birds and muskrats, and that its south fork is non-existent. Sure, there's a green sign beside the road south of Strachan directing you to the "South Fork," but you won't find those words on a map. The "fork" is actually Vetch Creek, which harbors its own population of small browns, brookies, and mountain whitefish. If you're into flyrodding along a tiny brook trimmed with willows and wild rose bushes (Alberta's pink-blossomed floral emblem), then Vetch Creek is definitely worth a look.

* * *

I awoke suddenly when something thudded on the canopy of my pickup. It was cold—early September—and my breath formed milky clouds of vapor as I stared at the fiberglass roof from the warmth of a down sleeping bag. The

The banks along Prairie Creek are a coniferous graveyard of sorts, the deadfall and log jams providing ideal cover for trout.

roof was covered in frosty condensation; the silhouettes of spruce trees were visible against the gray dawn sky outside the windows. *Thud!* I jolted upright, glancing around the truck for the source of the commotion. Satisfied that a bear hadn't decided to play the bongo on my roof, I opened the canopy hatch, leaned on the tailgate, and peered on top of the truck. Two or three brown cones lay like scaly turds in the twilight. And then I heard it—the frenzied chattering. I looked up just in time to see another two-inch cone come plunging down, a brown bomb dropped by a red squirrel. I raised a white undershirt in surrender before slipping it on. Then I got up to light a fire and put my dented aluminum coffee pot on the propane stove.

After breakfast I drove to a stretch of Prairie Creek east of Cow Lake off the Everdell Road. The landowner waved his arm in a sweeping gesture when I asked if I could fish there, his diesel tractor belching black smoke as it idled in the background. (Farmers always get off their machinery to talk to you: it's a good excuse to stretch their legs, and the last thing they want is some city dude leaning against the wrong moving part.) Basically, he gave me permission to fish anywhere I wanted on his land.

"Just remember to shut the gates," he added, hopping back onto his modern-day steed. Wires dangled from the tractor's engine, and I recalled a newspaper story I'd read about a Russian poacher who went fishing with a live electric cable. Seems everything went according to plan until the twenty-five-year-old waded into the pond to collect his booty. He'd forgotten to disconnect the wire. The man's death, I imagine, was spastic and quick.

A moderate breeze rustled the aspen leaves, and the blue sky was cloudless. Grasshopper weather—or so you'd think. There weren't many naturals around, and I figured the heavy frost had probably done most of them in. Undeterred, I tied on a size 8 red-bodied Stimulator. Although I rarely fish blind for brown trout with dry flies, I made an exception. I had a feeling the trout had seen enough hoppers that summer to remember the struggling legs, the neon bellies. Wading upstream, I cast the Stimulator onto every likely piece of holding water. The first brown rose from behind a tan boulder, fit for battle with polished gold gill plates and rakish white teeth. It measured sixteen inches. The next brown rose through a glassy seam between faster currents. I used a pile cast to buy a second or two of drag-free drift, and the fifteen-inch trout took the fly just before the bellying line would have yanked it downstream.

While a novice flyfisher might find Prairie Creek's browns intimidating, the creek nonetheless affords a beginning angler the ideal natural laboratory in which to observe trout behavior. For example, the browns are *exactly* where the fishing texts say they should be—log jams, deadfall, undercut banks, pockets, and pools. If you don't believe it, just hang around Prairie Creek during a good evening caddisfly hatch and watch for the dimpling riseforms that give away the trout's locations.

I spotted a brown of at least twenty-five inches rising next to the bank one evening just below the bridge at Terratima Lodge. I couldn't cover the fish because I'm not a skilled enough caster with my left hand, but I know it was huge because I crept through the grass to glimpse it. The leviathan brown held in the lee of a spruce root ball that had tumbled into the creek. A struggling caddisfly brought the trout to the surface, and even though the western sky was darkening, I could see the massive hooked kype on the male brown's lower jaw. When I tried—still laying down—to flick a dry fly and the last six feet of leader onto the surface, the trout vanished. Just like that. Gone.

*   *   *

One word describes Prairie Creek: quirky. Even during the lowest flows late in the season, the water is never colorless.

The air was humid that night as I drove west, back to the campground. The silhouette of a deer bounded across the highway, perfectly outlined against the purple sky. A few moments later the silhouette of a coyote followed. The countryside was full of dusky, evening smells that I either didn't notice during the day, when sight is paramount, or chose to ignore—pungent wood smoke rising from a sheet metal stovepipe, rotting marsh vegetation, freshly mown hay. My high beams illuminated a fluorescent orange traffic sign with black lettering: *Gravel Windrow.* How many of those can there be? The campground was deserted as I pulled into my prepaid site. The squirrels had retreated come nightfall, but I knew they'd be back at dawn. I parked as far away from the trees as I could.

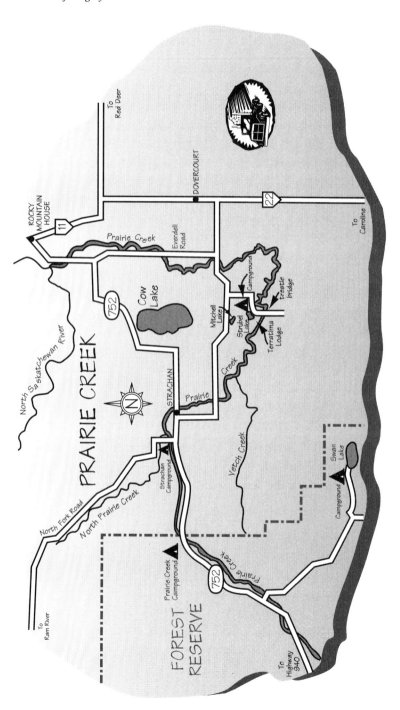

When You Go

Getting There

From Calgary, take Highway 2 north for about ninety miles to the junction with Highway 11; then drive west for about forty-five miles until you come to Rocky Mountain House. Follow the signs to Secondary Highway 752. Drive southwest for about fifteen miles to the Strachan Campground on Prairie Creek's center fork.

River Access

There's good access at the Strachan Campground. The Rocky Mountains Forest Reserve boundary is another five miles west along Secondary Highway 752, which parallels the center fork. Just inside the boundary there's another provincial day-use site and campground, but anglers can venture anywhere they want inside the forest reserve.

Because almost all of lower Prairie Creek flows through private land, access is restricted to bridges, road allowances, and cooperative landholders. (Keep in mind, however, that because the creek's banks are often overgrown and impenetrable, it's often impossible to stay below the high-water mark as required by Alberta law.) The best public access to this stretch is at the green trestle bridge beside Terratima Lodge, immediately south of Strubel Lake. The landowners on the east side of the bridge have fenced off a Buck for Wildlife section along some of the best brown trout habitat in the creek.

Equipment

I prefer a short rod for the upper creek—something about eight-feet long, maybe a three- or four-weight. A rod like that is perfect for the willowy, deadfall-ridden tucks and curves of the center fork, where a typical cast will be less than twenty feet. Hip waders are all you'll need. If it's a nice day, I usually wade wet in felt-soled boots. (I fish this stream from the bank ninety-five percent of the time anyway.)

Once the forks join and Prairie Creek flows past Terratima Lodge, the average depth and current speed make chest waders a necessity on all but the warmest days. Likewise, you'll want to use a bigger rod there as well, perhaps a nine-foot, four- or five-weight. I usually fish with at least a twelve-foot leader on these middle and lower reaches, because the brown trout are larger and more selective than the smallish brookies and browns in the upper creek. Tippet material should range from 2X for fall and winter streamer fishing to 7X for delicate dry fly presentations. (Tippets smaller than 7X are marketed by Madison Avenue yuppies who catch more stares than fish; leave the 8X material on the store shelves where it belongs, catching suckers.)

As for clothing, pack the usual compliment of southern Alberta outerwear, including rain gear, a warm jacket, a wide-brimmed hat, and polarized sunglasses.

Fly Patterns

Bring the same assortment of flies to Prairie Creek that you'd take to the North Raven River. (See the Fly Patterns listing in the chapter on the North Raven.) One additional pattern should be added to that list: the Grizzly Wulff in sizes 10 to 16. It's a great yellow-bodied imitation of the sulphur duns that hatch in June on Prairie Creek, and you'll want to have a few in your vest.

Seasons and Tactics

Angling is currently permitted year-round on Prairie Creek. (Some authorities are lobbying for a fall closure to protect the spawning browns.) As guide Ron Manz points out, underground springs keep large tracts of the creek ice-free all winter, so there's usually some open water between the snowdrifts. The trout congregate in deep, slow-moving pools at this time; try fishing a weighted black Woolly Bugger or Montana nymph, sizes 4 to 10. A winter flyfishing technique I've found effective is to nymph with a streamer. Use a floating line and indicator, but instead of stripping the streamer, let it dead-drift along the bottom. Big trout get lethargic in the off-season (just like big flyrodders), and while they're less likely to chase a streamer down, a brown might hit a Woolly Bugger that bumps it on the nose.

If you get a hankering to fish Prairie Creek during February, March, or April, keep an eye out for a relatively uncommon (at least in Alberta) species of small stonefly known as the early brown stone. This is one of the few early-spring hatches that will get the trout's attention. Imitate the insect by casting a size 12 brown Elk Hair Caddis along the banks and through the pockets. By late spring and early summer, Prairie Creek is one of central Alberta's most reliable dry-fly streams (assuming, of course, that run-off is low and it's fishable). Sometime about mid-May, the salmonflies and golden stones will start coming off. During peak years, Prairie Creek's salmonfly emergence can rival that of the Crowsnest River.

If the water's clear, June usually features thick hatches of sulphur mayflies, which prefer the faster, broken currents of the middle and upper creek. The best thing about sulphurs is that they emerge at midday, making them the perfect antidote to a hangover. A short-lived brown drake hatch reportedly takes place on lower Prairie Creek sometime in early July, but I've yet to witness it. Brown drakes hatch after dark in slow, silt-bottomed water. More reliable and consistently productive are the caddisfly hatches that occur throughout the summer and into the fall. The best emergences are after sunset, and that's when the creek's trophy browns—four pounds and up—leave their bankside hollows to check out the neighborhood. Watch carefully for their stealthy, dimpling rises.

Pale morning duns hatch sporadically during the daytime in July. August features tremendous grasshopper fishing along the creek's tangled banks, especially on windy afternoons. Splat a Letort Hopper or Stimulator pattern down hard, twitching the fly slightly to impart a little motion. The ubiquitous blue-winged olives start showing up in good numbers again in September, and that's also a good time to start throwing big streamers to moody brown trout with sex on their minds. Unlike the aforementioned winter technique, strip these streamers back as fast as you can.

Special Regulations

None, really—at least as far as the flyrodder is concerned. Prairie Creek is open all year; the legal limit is five trout.

"I want to see some regulation changes, and if we have to publicize the creek to get those changes, then so be it," Ron Manz told me. "At a minimum, the creek should be shut down in the late fall for spawning and not reopened until late spring to allow the trout to disperse to their summer habitat." I couldn't agree more, and it's troubling to think that provincial officials don't feel the same way. The only thing saving Prairie Creek to date is the cautious nature of the wild browns, which exercise better judgment than the Alberta environment minister.

Places to Stay and Eat

Terratima Lodge is a top-notch facility with streamside access to some of the best fishing on Prairie Creek. Accommodations vary from rustic cabins sleeping between two and twelve people to the new Wolf Willow Lodge, a two-story log building with ten double rooms. Terratima's property also borders Strubel Lake, which offers great flyfishing for rainbows to five pounds. Terratima hosts Larry and Claire Kennedy can be reached at Box 1636, Rocky Mountain House, Alta., Canada, T0M 1T0 or telephone 403-845-6786 or 403-845-2444 (fax).

There are several good hotels, motels, and restaurants in Rocky Mountain House. Contact the Chamber of Commerce (Box 1374, Rocky Mountain House, Alta., Canada, T0M 1T0; 403-845-5450). If you'd rather camp, both the Strachan and Prairie Creek campgrounds along Secondary Highway 752 are well-maintained and right beside the water. There are also campgrounds at Strubel and Mitchell Lakes.

Guides and Outfitters

Once again, Ron Manz at Before the Hatch Anglers (Box 2304, Rocky Mountain House, Alta., Canada, T0M 1T0; 403-845-4435) is pretty much it as far as local guiding is concerned. You may also contact him through Ram River Sports at 403-845-4160. Calgary's Bow River Troutfitters (2122 Crowchild Trail N.W., Calgary, Alta., Canada, T2M 3Y7; 403-282-8868; bowriver@flyshop.com) is starting to guide in this area as well.

Other Attractions

The Prairie Creek region features mountain biking, horseback riding, bird-watching, and whitewater rafting on the upper Red Deer River. Inquire at Terratima Lodge or through the Rocky Mountain House Chamber of Commerce (address and telephone number given above). For things to do in and around Rocky Mountain House, refer to the Other Attractions listing in the chapter on the North Raven River.

10
North Ram River

The cutthroat is often depicted as a stupid fish that feeds recklessly and doesn't present the same sporting opportunity as, say, rainbow or brown trout. I think that's utter hogwash. True, cutthroat are less selective than other trout, mainly because they inhabit cold headwaters where food is at a premium and the growing season short. In essence, they take what they can get, when they can get it. Remind yourself of that the next time you're lunging for the hors d'oeuvre tray at a cocktail party—people who feed opportunistically are said to have hearty appetites, but we rarely dismiss them as simple-minded.

Unfortunately, where the cutthroats' range overlaps that of Homo sapiens—which is just about everywhere nowadays—the trout's opportunistic feeding habits have often been their downfall. Such is the case on the North Ram River in west-central Alberta. The North Ram has been managed as the province's premier catch-and-release fishery since 1981, but the well-intentioned regulations have exacted a price from the wild cutthroats. Each time I fish there the evidence presents itself anew: jaws so badly hook-scarred they look like the track-ridden arms of a junkie; a netted trout that has your fly lodged in one side of its mouth and an H & L Variant in the other side, tippet dangling like a dog's broken leash; a disfigured upper lip where a fishing line has sliced through half an inch of flesh; mandibles torn by the careless removal of hooks.

These are the legacies of mandatory catch-and-release fishing. I release almost all the fish I catch, and I understand that catch-and-release is an important management tool, but flyfishers who use the catch-and-release ethic as a shield to deflect criticism (or as a narcotic to assuage the remorse of wrenching a fish from its environment into theirs) are kidding themselves. Any trout that's been yanked from the water ten times in one summer is probably better off in a frying pan.

"It makes for some awkward picture-taking," guide Ron Manz acknowledged, cradling a bronze-cheeked, eighteen-inch cutthroat in his hands during a trip last summer. "You always have to be conscious of the best side to put forward." Ron's best side is his good-natured, no-nonsense approach to flyfishing. With a jaw like Harrison Ford's and a preference for split-cane rods, Ron realizes that the North Ram is, as Steven J. Meyers phrased it in *San Juan River Chronicle*, "a river in danger of being loved to death, for all the right reasons."

*   *   *

One of those reasons was headed downstream with fifty feet of fly line trailing from its mouth. I'd hooked the cutthroat on an Irresistible, and the tip of my four-weight rod was trying to touch its butt as the line shot through the guides. The trout stopped and swung into a small pocket of water along the bank; I reeled like mad as I walked toward the fish along a gravel fan. As I came within twenty feet of the cutthroat, I noticed a metallic flash at the corner of its jaw, and it saddened me to think that I'd find a Mepps spinner in the mouth of the biggest trout I'd hooked all day. When I got closer, however, I realized that the flash wasn't a lure at all, but the chrome guide and last four inches of my fly rod, which had broken off and slid down the line until reaching the trout's mouth. Suddenly, landing the fish became more important, because I knew the folks at the Sage factory would be a lot quicker to believe my story if I had the broken tip to send in along with the rest of the rod. Thankfully, the trout made a couple of short darts and then succumbed. I walked upstream to join Ron at the next pool. He took one look at the busted tip in my fingers and said, "That must have been a good one."

Ron and I had been trying to get together on the North Ram for months. Finally, during the second week of September, we made plans to meet at Rocky Mountain House and drive the hour or so west to the river. One of the things that protects the North Ram is that it's at least a three-hour drive from either Calgary or Edmonton, the two largest cities in Alberta. As a result, the North Ram is primarily a weekend destination, and if you can manage to slip away during the week, there's still a good chance you'll have large sections of the river to yourself. To *ensure* we'd have the river to ourselves, Ron showed up at our cafe rendezvous towing an Argo 8x8 on a trailer behind his truck.

The Argo is an all-terrain vehicle, and true to its billing, it's got eight-wheel-drive. You can mount an outboard motor on its green transom, but even without the motor the Argo can still cross lakes and slow-moving rivers, propelled by the webbed treads on its bulbous rubber tires.

"I can't imagine a better duck blind," Ron said, as we clambered over rocks and logs on the five-mile trail leading to a remote stretch of the North Ram. "You just drive wherever you want in the marsh, pour the coffee, and wait for the birds." We didn't have to wait long before Ron came to a halt and pointed at a ruffed grouse preening itself beneath a spruce tree. Ebony, Ron's black cocker spaniel, jumped out of the Argo and gave chase.

The weather was drizzly and cool. The trembling aspens, which had begun to change color, were warm yellow splotches on an otherwise dreary day. We used the Argo as an amphibious variation of a drift boat, following the river downstream for several miles and getting out to fish the good water. The river's monochrome surface looked brittle, like smoked glass. There were no fish rising—no bugs to be seen—so I selected a Beadhead Prince Nymph to try. A couple of feet above the fly, I attached a half-inch piece of fluorescent green yarn to the leader with a slip knot. I chose the yarn because I wanted an especially bright indicator. The fly hadn't been in the water ten seconds when the first cutthroat swung at the nymph. I saw the white gape of its mouth followed by a silver flash, but pulled the nymph away before the

Cutthroat trout are less selective than other trout, mainly because they inhabit cold headwaters, like those of the North Ram River, where food is at a premium and the growing season short.

barbless hook could penetrate. I cussed to myself and glanced downstream at Ron, who was already tight to a thrashing cutthroat.

We leapfrogged up the river from pool to pool and then decided to take turns at a particularly enticing corner. I'd catch a trout and then Ron would catch a trout. While he fished, I sipped on a Coke; while I fished, he puffed on a cigarette. We both took lots of pictures.

"You're up," I'd say, pressuring a cutthroat into swimming downstream so Ron could get into casting position.

"Yup."

The drizzle let up by midafternoon, and a small mayfly, which neither of us could identify, started hatching . It didn't matter, because a size 16 Irresistible was close enough to fool the trout. Once we'd cast to all the rising fish in a pool, we'd back up and work through it again with nymphs. Ron puzzled for thirty minutes over one trout he could see feeding on the bottom before it finally took a size 18 olive Hare's Ear. After landing the fish, he turned to me and grinned, "And people say cutthroats can't be difficult."

*   *   *

As I've said, the odd cutthroat notwithstanding, the most difficult part of flyfishing the North Ram is getting there. The only vehicle access is by gravel road, and that in itself is enough to dissuade some city dwellers.

The river bottom is gravel as well. On a bright summer afternoon, the stones shine in a hundred hues of brown, gold, beige, and pewter. Hovering above those stones are cutthroats averaging fourteen to sixteen inches in length, with some up to twenty inches.

"We have everything here," Ron boasted, referring not only to the North Ram but also to the myriad streams and lakes within an hour's drive. "There's brown trout, there's bull trout, there's cutthroat, there's rainbows—we even have golden trout. Very few golden trout, but they're here."

The North Ram is just small enough to wade easily; you can cross back and forth pretty much anywhere but the pools. Because much of the river flows through a wide flood plain, there's typically lots of room to cast. In fact, the North Ram reminds me of some of the freestone rivers on New Zealand's South Island, where I spent four months exploring the watersheds a few years ago. The North Ram's pools and runs are textbook perfect, and by midsummer the clarity of the water approaches that of the New Zealand

The North Ram's pools and runs are textbook perfect, and by midsummer the water clarity approaches that of New Zealand rivers.

rivers as well. You can also expect to do a lot of walking between productive water at the North Ram—again, just like New Zealand.

*   *   *

It was the end of July—hot—and because I knew I'd be doing a lot of walking, I placed a can of Coke in the river. I built a little dam out of some stones in a backwater along the bank and watched the can bob in the impoundment as cold water flushed against the red and white logo. I fixed the can's position by crude triangulation—a downed tree, a spruce-covered hill, a bend in the river. I walked upstream and noticed a big green drake as it floated around an eddy three times, skittering and fluttering. There were no takers. Not a good sign.

Something moved in the willows to my right—something big—and I thought *bear!* But it wasn't a bear, just a cow. A brown and white Hereford, one of dozens allowed along the river because of a provincial government grazing lease.

"They just destroy the aesthetics of the west country when you take somebody out there," Ron once told me. "Some of my clients who live in the big city find the cows entertaining, but to me they're depressing." Me, too.

More uplifting was the bright common red paintbrush in the forest openings, used by Indians to stimulate urination and treat internal bleeding. There was white common yarrow, purple-stemmed aster, and mattes of clover with bees hovering over the rounded white flowers. A pair of common ravens croaked from a bluff across the river, and I reached for the compact binoculars I carry with me while fishing. In addition to birdwatching, I use them to scan the water for rising fish. The ravens were hopping up and down, their black shaggy throat feathers clearly visible through the binoculars. Many naturalists consider ravens the most intelligent birds in the world, pointing out that ravens have a greater variety of calls than any animal except humans. In his book *Ravens In Winter*, Bernd Heinrich relates how mountaineers on Alaska's Mount Denali (Mount McKinley) have declared ravens a pest. Seems the birds have learned to associate the small red flags used to mark climbers' food caches with easy pickings. Some ravens have even been spotted digging through three feet of snow 10,000 feet up the mountain to get at a cache.

I cast a size 12 Royal Trude into a pool, and a fourteen-inch cutthroat rose through three feet of water to take the fly. A little farther upstream I saw another trout rise next to the dark trunk of a fallen spruce tree. When I cast the Trude within a foot of the tree, the fish darted out, hit the fly, struggled, and swam back under the tree. My line was taut—unmoving. When I walked up to where the cutthroat had disappeared, I could see the fly two feet beneath the surface, but now it was lodged in a branch and not in the trout's jaw. I dunked my bare arm up to the shirt sleeve and wriggled the fly free.

Continuing up the river, I came to a mossy cliff rising straight out of the water. The moss was orange and yellow—out of place against the gray rock and dark green forest—and my eyes were drawn to it the same way they are drawn to the reddish-orange slashes beneath a cutthroat's gills. When you hold a cutthroat in your hand, black spots sprinkled across its back like pepper, it's the crimson lower jaw that inevitably catches your eye.

Around the next bend I spotted four fish rising in a narrow run between a downed spruce tree and the bank. The trout were taking pale morning duns, and I tied on a Sulphur Sparkle Dun and proceeded to catch them one by one, starting with the fish farthest downstream. Recalling my earlier encounter with the cutthroat that threw the Royal Trude, as soon as each

Around the bend, four fish rose to pale morning duns in a narrow run between a downed spruce tree and the bank.

trout took the fly I applied pressure to force the fish downstream, clear of the sunken tree. Besides, that way the hooked trout didn't have a chance to disturb the cutthroats still rising. I landed three of the four fish—they measured fifteen, seventeen, and eighteen inches.

By late afternoon I'd caught about ten trout and decided to call it a day. During a heavy hatch of golden stones, a flyrodder can catch that many cutthroats in a single pool on the North Ram, but on average, a dozen fish landed is a pretty good outing. I wandered downstream in search of the Coke, a tired angler in need of a drink. I couldn't find it. The landmarks seemed blurrier than they had that morning; there were lots of bends in the river, lots of spruce-covered hills. I asked myself what Al Unser, Jr. would have done, running out of gas because he couldn't find the pits. I looked for the Coke for fifteen minutes, and then decided to call off the search. No doubt another angler would find it in due course. Lifting the pop can to his lips, he'd chuckle at the simple-minded person who had left it behind, then opportunistically slake his thirst.

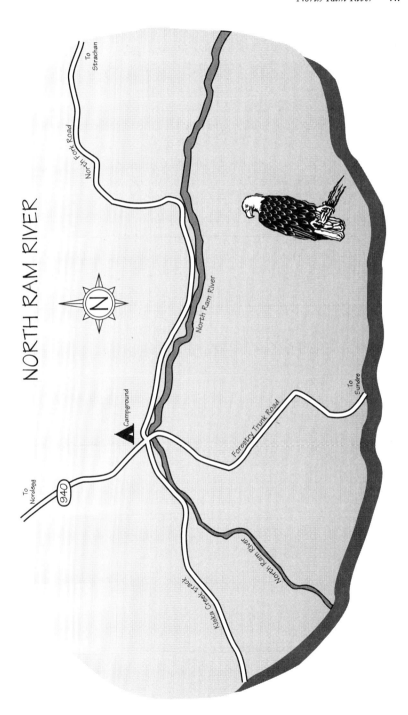

NORTH RAM RIVER

N

To Strachan

North Fork Road

North Ram River

Campground

To Nordegg

940

Forestry Trunk Road

To Sundre

North Ram River

Kista Creek track

When You Go

Getting There

The easiest way to reach the North Ram River from Calgary is via Rocky Mountain House. Drive north from Calgary on Highway 2 for about ninety miles to the junction with Highway 11. Head west for about forty-five miles until you come to Rocky Mountain House; then continue west on Highway 11 for fifty-five miles until you reach Nordegg. Just west of town, drive south on Highway 940 (also known as the Forestry Trunk Road) for about twenty-three miles until the road crosses the North Ram.

River Access

A good gravel road follows the river for eight miles downstream of the Highway 940 bridge crossing. Since the entire North Ram watershed is in the Rocky Mountains Forest Reserve, access is unlimited. Nevertheless, keep in mind that the river receives a lot of angling pressure, and the best flyfishing is generally found as far away from the road as you can get.

Equipment

Regardless of what the weather's doing in Calgary or elsewhere in southern Alberta, bring plenty of warm clothing to the North Ram. It can really sock in there, and many are the days that I've started fishing in bright sunlight and finished in a downpour. Consequently, you should also come equipped with chest waders, rain gear, a hat, polarized sunglasses, and felt-soled wading boots.

As for rods, you'll want anything from a four- to a six-weight, depending on conditions and whether you intend to cast dries, nymphs, or streamers. My all-round choice would be a nine-foot, five-weight, though I have to confess that for the most part I find myself using a nine-foot, four-weight Sage RPL. As mentioned, I rarely fish for cutthroats with streamers or heavily-weighted nymphs, and I find the stiffer graphite on the Sage four-weight more than adequate for casting even the bulkiest dry flies. I use a floating fly line ninety-five percent of the time on the North Ram, but if you decide to cast a streamer, a sink-tip line will get the fly down quicker.

Leaders should be between seven-and-a-half and twelve feet; 3X or 4X tippets will fool all but the most selective trout in the North Ram. (Just in case, bring along some 5X as well.)

Fly Patterns

When it comes to dries, I prefer buoyant, highly visible attractor patterns on the choppy freestone water of the North Ram. Try Lime Trudes, Royal Wulffs, Yellow Humpies, Stimulators, and Letort Hoppers in sizes 8 to 14. Good caddis imitations are Elk Hair and Goddard caddis (sizes 10 to 18). For smaller mayflies, try Irresistibles, Borger Yarn Wing Duns, and H & L Variants (sizes 12 to 18). Larger mayflies like the green drakes can be imitated with Olive or Gray Wulffs, sizes 10 to 14.

Effective nymph patterns include Gold-ribbed Hare's Ear (sizes 8 to 18), Beadhead Prince (sizes 10 to 16), Zug Bugs (sizes 10 to 14), and Brooks' Golden Stone and Montana nymphs (sizes 4 to 10). As far as streamers are concerned, guide Ron Manz recommends the Kiwi Muddler with black, white, or natural brown rabbit wings in sizes 6 to 10.

Seasons and Tactics

Because the North Ram doesn't drain as far back into the Rocky Mountains as other foothills streams, spring rains—and not snowmelt—usually determine the amount of run-off each year. During a dry spring, the river can be in great shape by the time the season opens in mid-June. On the other hand, if those April showers turn into a three-month ordeal, chances are the North Ram won't be fishable until July. Either way, the first big insects to watch for are the stoneflies.

"Golden stones are our biggest hatch, no question," Ron said. Their emergence varies from year to year according to the water condition and temperature. The biggest hatches will generally be in June and July, but golden stones are often found along the North Ram well into August. There's nothing subtle about fishing to trout rising to stoneflies. Don't be afraid to lay the artificial down hard, skimming it across the surface if necessary. If golden stones are egg-laying but the cutthroats aren't rising to them, try nymphing with a Brooks' Golden Stone, weighting the fly so it tumbles along the bottom.

I often fish blind with attractor dry flies and have great success during the early season, concentrating on the obvious pools. The trout are less wary at this time of the year. The best bet is to start casting at the tail of a pool and methodically work your way to the head. As the season progresses and the number of anglers on the river increases, the cutthroats become pickier. By late summer and fall, it might even be necessary to match specific hatches.

As Ron put it, "Some of these fish are being caught and released many times in a season, and they're getting a lot smarter. They're not feeding as actively on the surface now as they did, say, five or six years ago." Green drakes and pale morning duns are among several species of mayflies that hatch on the North Ram—the PMDs throughout July and August, the green drakes primarily in July but also into August. A small population of caddis-flies hatch throughout the summer and fall.

If the cutthroat aren't responding to dry flies, try tying a weighted Zug Bug or Gold-ribbed Hare's Ear Nymph on a dropper a couple of feet below an attractor dry, which then serves as the indicator. (See the Seasons & Tactics section in the chapter on the North Raven River for more details.) If the trout *still* aren't hitting, change to a standard nymph rig and work the fly along the pool bottoms.

You should also keep in mind that as the trout receive more and more angling pressure during the course of the season, they're apt to leave the pools and move into less-obvious lies that most flyfishers would overlook—small pockets behind boulders, narrow current seams along the banks, and under and around fallen trees in the river.

During the fall, when the sun is lower in the sky and the forest a leafy patchwork of yellows and greens and reds, the best dry-fly fishing occurs later in the day. This is the time of year to watch for blue-winged olives; they emerge best on the North Ram, as elsewhere, on dreary, overcast afternoons.

Special Regulations

The North Ram has been managed as Alberta's premier catch-and-release cut-throat fishery since 1981. The season runs from June 16 to October 31, and all anglers must use barbless hooks.

Places to Stay and Eat

There's motel accommodation and a couple of decent truck stop-type restaurants in Nordegg, but for anything fancy you're going to have to head to Rocky Mountain House. Contact the chamber of commerce there at: Box 1374, Rocky Mountain House, Alta., Canada, T0M 1T0; 403-845-5450.

If you prefer to camp, there's a serviced campground at the junction of the North Ram River and the Forestry Trunk Road. Primitive campsites can also be found over the length of the river, and there are additional provincial campgrounds at Nordegg if the North Ram site is full.

Guides and Outfitters

I personally recommend Ron Manz at Before the Hatch Anglers (Box 2304, Rocky Mountain House, Alta., Canada, T0M 1T0; 403-845-4435) or through Ram River Sports (403-845-4160). Ron also offers walk-and-wade fishing on numerous streams in the area, float tube fishing on alpine lakes, and heli-fishing in the South Ram River canyon, one of the most spectacular and inaccessible angling destinations in the province.

A few Calgary guides also offer multi-day trips to the North Ram. Try Brian Anderson (403-249-8978) or Mike Day at Bow River Troutfitters (2122 Crowchild Trail, N.W., Calgary, Alta., Canada, T2M 3Y7; 403-282-8868; bowriver@flyshop.com).

Other Attractions

For things to do in and around Rocky Mountain House, see the Other Attractions listing in Chapter 8 on the North Raven River.

11
Red Deer River

I have a thing for underdogs: ravens that scavenge at the edges of civilization, as comfortable atop an Iceland dump as they are atop a Texas mesquite thicket; coyotes that wander the margins of our fields, ruffled and wary; five-foot-four point guards on college basketball teams.

Alberta flyfishers have their own underdog to champion—the goldeye. No, it's not a trout, or a char, or a bass. The point is, who cares? Goldeye will take artificial flies, both wet and dry; they jump; and they fight admirably, angling their thin but deep bodies against the current like silver rudders. E. Donnall Thomas, Jr., in his book *Whitefish Can't Jump & Other Tales of Gamefish On The Fly*, writes, "I've never really understood why the goldeye hasn't attracted more attention as a gamefish. They're not large, of course, averaging a pound or so, but their aggressive character seems fair compensation for their lack of size."

Okay, let's face it. Goldeye aren't popular because they thrive in dirty water and warm places. As humans, we have an aversion to dirty water based on the fact that drinking it can kill us. Warm places aren't as troublesome since the advent of ceiling fans and air conditioning, but flyfishers steeped in trout snobbery still associate cacti with a place they'd rather not be.

Well, the purists be damned! The Red Deer River valley is my kind of place, the goldeye is my kind of fish. Goldeye come from the scientific order *Osteoglossiformes*, derived from the Greek word *osteon*, which means "bone." The goldeye and its close relative, the mooneye, are the only living representatives of this order in North America. The other 215 species of freshwater bony fish inhabit tropical waters in northern Australia, Africa, and southeast Asia. In appearance, goldeye have been compared to shad and miniature tarpon. Both descriptions are accurate. They are metallic blue on the back, silver on the sides, white on the belly. They have sharp teeth on the jaws and tongue, large scales, and a blunt nose. Yet the single distinguishing feature, as you'd expect, is a black pupil encircled by a gold iris. The eye is visually arresting—the sort of eye that catches your gaze and raises more questions than it answers.

*   *   *

I stared into the fish's eye as it lay in the net. The evening sun was minutes away from slipping behind a canyon wall. The stratified rock of the badlands looked like a faded rainbow snipped from the sky and draped across the creased and folded landforms. Umbers. Ochers. Siennas. Earthy pigments laid down millions of years ago as sediment, now compressed into horizontal layers of coal, sandstone, mudstone, and ironstone. The fourteen-inch goldeye flopped in my hand as I pried the hook from its jaw, its silver scales glowing in the slanted light.

Badlands result when wind and water erode soft rock strata into sculpted bluffs and gullies, fantastically-formed buttes, and mushroom-shaped hoodoos. Seventy-five million years ago, during the late Cretaceous period, these badlands, which extend through much of southern Alberta along the Red Deer River valley, were at the edge of a vast inland sea. Dinosaurs roamed among ferns and swamp cypress; oysters and clams thrived in beds of sand. How strange, I thought, placing the goldeye back into the water, to be walking on the fossils of marine invertebrates 600 miles from the nearest ocean. The goldeye darted away; I picked up my fly rod and waded back into the pool.

Where there's one goldeye, there's always another. They migrate upriver in huge schools, beginning their journey from Lake Diefenbaker in the neighboring province of Saskatchewan, a lake that is hundreds of miles downstream.

"When we get a great big flush of mud through here, they come all the way up from the lake," said Doug Wood, an avid flyrodder who owns a fishing shop in the city of Red Deer. By midsummer, goldeye are resident throughout the lower Red Deer River drainage. They're also found in other Alberta river systems, including the South Saskatchewan, lower Oldman, lower Bow, Athabasca, Peace, and North Saskatchewan. However, to me, goldeye are synonymous with the badlands (both fish and landscape undeservedly maligned), and that's where I almost always flyfish for them.

The water in the pool was so muddy I couldn't see the river bottom through eight inches of current. I was fishing just downstream of Dry Island Buffalo Jump Provincial Park, east of Trochu. Goldeye holes are hard to miss. The first giveaway are the whittled sticks poked in the ground along a bank. They're used to prop up fishing rods, of course, though some will undoubtedly be charred from double duty as spits for roasting walleye caught in the same holes. Look for beer cans, too, sometimes laying next to small plastic bags with labels like "Pickerel Rig" or "Jim's Bait Shop." And whereas the dinosaur bones entombed in the badlands can surface just about anywhere, the skeletons at goldeye holes are generally found in the black ashes of an abandoned fire pit and may contain bits of rotting flesh clinging to a piscine head. The water at these holes will typically be flowing upstream, forming a whirlpool at the edge of the river's main flow and reminding you of a stirred cup of coffee with globs of curdled cream spinning on top.

I resumed casting a size 8 Woolly Worm. The trick was to cast well upstream, into the head of the eddy, letting the sink-tip line take the bushy fly down a few feet as it swung past me. Goldeye will slash recklessly at a dry fly, but beneath the surface they are often more deliberate, and the wise angler will set the hook at the first pause in the retrieve. Set the hook hard, because a goldeye has a mouth like an athletic supporter. You want to drive the hook home and hang on, but flyrodders should still expect to lose as many goldeye as they land. A whopping specimen will go eighteen inches. Most fish will be between ten and fifteen.

When I'd caught about a dozen goldeye out of the same pool, when the last strands of pink and purple cloud had dissipated and the stars had blinked on one by one, I walked the quarter-mile along the river back to the provincial park. A gibbous moon slowly rose across the river valley. I could hear goldeye continuing to rise as I crested a bluff, leaving the river and its skeletons to creatures better equipped for darkness than myself.

*   *   *

Discovering the badlands from either an eastern or western approach is stupefying. One moment you're driving past grain fields and duck-covered potholes, the next moment you're overlooking an abyss up to 500 feet deep and one mile wide. I find it unnerving to view such relief from *above*—no doubt a consequence of having grown up near the mountains, where the tendency is to stare up at the grandeur and down at your *feet*.

If you're driving to the badlands from Calgary, keep an eye out for the pale blue water tower perched above the town of Three Hills. Not far from the tower is the Dairy King, where for a couple of bucks a waitress will hand you a milkshake so thick that sucking it up a straw will jeopardize the blood vessels in your tongue.

Red Deer River goldeye take artificial flies, both wet and dry, aggressively. They jump and fight admirably.

Unfortunately, such luxuries weren't available to the homesteaders who settled along the river at the turn of the century, spreading like acne across the face of the badlands. They sought out seepages and pockets of trees to shelter their log homes, and several of these pioneer cabins still stand. One of the most interesting is located on the right bank three miles below Dry Island Buffalo Jump Provincial Park, its door decorated with cattle brands popular at the time of its construction. However, coal mining quickly displaced ranching as the economic mainstay of the Drumheller area, and at one time over forty mines operated up and down the valley. The discovery of oil in central Alberta in the 1940s spelled the end of the mining era, but the abandoned shafts and heaps of coal slag linger on. Ironically, Drumheller's economy is now largely fueled by tourists coming to gape at the mining relics and fossilized bones.

*   *   *

Yet there's more to the Red Deer River than badlands and goldeye. Farther upstream, west of Innisfail, wild brown trout have successfully been transplanted from the lower Bow River.

"We could have a better brown trout population here than the Bow," Wood once told me. "That's been proven." Although the Red Deer River browns are faring well, Wood said their numbers are still being held in check somewhat for two reasons: local anglers continue to kill brown trout despite mandatory catch-and-release regulations, and the browns have to compete with pike and walleye in the same watershed.

Nonetheless, I've spent several good days fishing for browns in the braided channels below Gleniffer Lake and the Dickson Dam. Autumn is the best time to go there. The trembling aspens will be changing color then, the gold-colored leaves spiraling onto slate-gray pools. Don't expect solitude, however, because the Red Deer's fall run of mountain whitefish draws anglers from throughout the province. Most of these folks come equipped with lawn chairs and white buckets—the limit is ten fish apiece—and they can stage quite a spectacle. Last fall I watched an elderly woman drag a twenty-inch whitefish onto a gravel bar, then swirl and shout at her husband, who was sitting about fifty yards downstream along the same bank.

"Harry!" she bellowed. When he didn't respond, she tried again. "Haaaarrrry!" Still no response. Now, Harry may have been tired of bonking his wife's fish on the head, or maybe he'd forgotten to turn his hearing aid on. Either way, Harry wasn't budging. Disgusted and muttering words I couldn't quite make out, Harry's wife flung her fishing rod on the ground and strode away toward her husband. The whitefish, meanwhile, continued to flop against the rocks, obviously suffering. I walked over to it, picked up a rock, and whacked it on the head. When I looked up, the man and woman had started briskly walking toward me. I'm sure they thought I was going to stuff the whitefish into my waders and make a run for it. When I stood up and they realized that wasn't the case, the couple noticeably slowed their pace. "Thanks," they said in unison, and I resisted an impulse to whack them with the dead whitefish.

Fortunately, the whitefish anglers usually mimic their quarry and travel in schools, and I never seem to have much trouble finding quiet spots to fish for brown trout. By October the browns are becoming territorial as they chase off all comers in preparation for spawning. That's the time to drag a size 4 silver Zonker along the streambed at the end of a 1X tippet.

"The browns in the Red Deer River like bottom stuff and minnows," Wood said. "By the time a fish reaches four pounds, caddisflies might not mean anything if it can catch a whitefish minnow once a day."

* * *

Ian Thomson had never fished for goldeye. Frankly, I doubt he'd ever thought about it. But one of the things I like best about Ian is his sense of adventure. So when I proposed a trip to the badlands last August, he bit. We hatched a scheme to float the river in kick boats. The Red Deer is slow-moving there, and I figured the kick boats would be perfect for getting up-close and intimate with the fish and the scenery. Because I intended to spend five days exploring the river north and south of Drumheller (Ian couldn't get away from the city for that long), we arranged to meet at the Tolman Bridge campground. He arrived on the appointed morning just as I was eating a bowl of cereal and admiring the sunrise. Since we planned to take out at the campground that evening, we loaded my fishing gear into Ian's 4x4 and drove to the put-in at the provincial park.

When we got there, Ian looked at the river and shook his head.

"Are you sure about this?" he asked, the brown water lapping against the green grass at his feet. It had been raining off and on for the past couple of days, and as I'd discovered prior to Ian's arrival, the Red Deer quickly muddies when cloudbursts flush silt and clay into the river. What I'd also discovered was that goldeye have no trouble spotting flies in murky water.

"Ian," I said, "trust me on this one. We're going to have a blast." The kick boats turned out to be the perfect craft for floating the river. I found it disconcerting that I couldn't see my white flippers dangling a foot beneath the surface, but once I overcame the anxiety, I settled in and enjoyed the ride. I stuck with the dependable Woolly Worm, while Ian tied on a size 6 black Woolly Bugger. We both caught fish—lots of them.

"Just had another goldfish on," Ian shouted from across the river.

"That's gold*eye*, Ian," I responded.

"Oh, right."

During the lulls, which were few, I tilted my head back and took in the rarefied scenery. There were narrow fringes of green vegetation on either side of the river—cottonwoods, willows, dogwoods, saskatoon bushes. Yet as soon as the land angled upward above the flood plain, the eroded badlands prevailed, largely barren save for the odd patch of greasewood or sage, some of these shrubs sheltering prairie rattlesnakes. In the strangling aridity of a wind-

Kick boats are perfect for getting up-close and intimate with the fish and the scenery of the slow-moving Red Deer River.

less afternoon, shade spells the difference between life and death in the badlands. Bank swallows wait out the heat in cliffside holes, mule deer lay in dusky ravines, and cottontail rabbits twitch in scraggly thickets. By day the sky belongs to golden eagles and ferruginous hawks, the parched soil to grasshoppers and their incessant thrum. As we drifted along I found myself staring at the turquoise pontoons on my kick boat and thinking how out of place they looked in the brown water and muted landscape.

"These goldeye fight fine until you get them close," Ian remarked, "then they sort of give up." He paused to sniff the air, bear-like, and glanced at his wrist.

"I think a storm's on its way," Ian said. "The barometer's falling like crazy." Ian has a thing for gadgets. One of his niftiest possessions is a wristwatch that records the barometric pressure. Because it also has a thermometer and is waterproof, in theory Ian could lay his watch on the bottom of a river to predict an emergence. There's a digital compass on the watch and an altimeter, which come in handy when you're following a topographic map and trying to find that alpine lake you overheard a drunk guide mention at the Trout Unlimited banquet. Oh, and if you're so inclined, Ian's watch also tells the time, though neither of us seem to care much about hours and minutes when we're knee-deep in a river.

I flipped through a catalog once that advertised Ian's watch as a "survival" item. Truth is, though I've yet to be saved by Ian's watch, it *has* come close to doing me in. A couple of years ago, I made the mistake of asking Ian the altitude while he drove along the lip of a hundred-foot escarpment.

"Uh, Ian," I said, the truck angling toward the abyss as Ian rolled back his sleeve, "we're going over the edge!"

"I know," he replied, distractedly pushing a button on his watch, "my wife's been saying the same thing for years."

Anyhow, when Ian says the barometer's falling like crazy, it's usually a pretty good indication to seek cover. Not twenty minutes after Ian's prognosis on the Red Deer that day, a gray smudge of cloud started building from the west, obscuring the sun. The river's surface teemed with rising goldeye. I'm a skeptic when it comes to lunar cycles and their impact on fishing, but I've seen too many feeding frenzies just before a storm to dismiss the influence of a rapidly falling barometer. We both tied on grasshopper imitations and both hooked one goldeye after another, staying within fifty feet of the nearest bank in case the storm turned electrical. When it did and when the rain obliterated any sign of rising fish, we hunkered beneath some willows and stared out from beneath the brims of our felt hats.

Years ago, at the turn of the century, it seemed the goldeye would be obliterated by human greed. Once abundant in Lake Winnipeg in the Canadian province of Manitoba, goldeye stocks were seriously depleted when English butcher Robert Firth discovered the value of smoke-curing the fish. In fact, smoked Winnipeg goldeye, dark orange in color, was soon being served on transcontinental trains to British royalty and American presidents. It's somewhat ironic, especially given the current popularity of the catch-and-release credo, that only in death did the goldeye gain the respect that eluded it in life.

If that's not the sign of an underdog, I'd like to know what is.

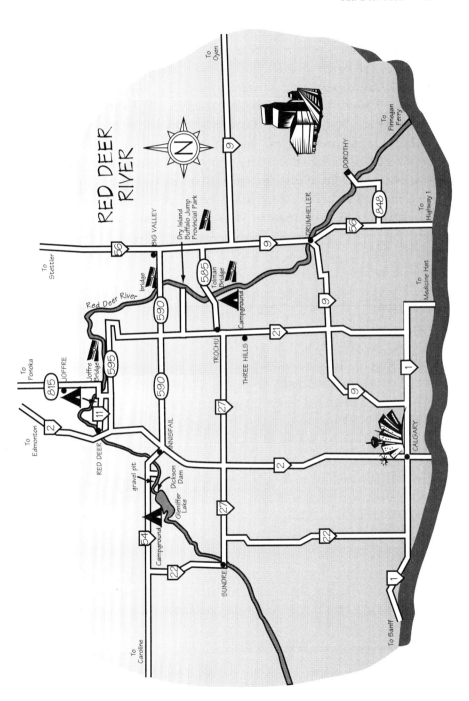

When You Go

Getting There

To reach the river west of Red Deer, drive north from Calgary on Highway 2 about seventy miles to Innisfail. Turn west on Highway 54, and you'll come to a bridge crossing the Red Deer River about three miles outside of town. The city of Red Deer is another twenty miles north of Innisfail on Highway 2.

The lower Red Deer River and the badlands are best reached by driving east from Calgary on Highway 1 for about fifteen miles and then heading north on Highway 9 for about sixty-five miles to Drumheller.

River Access

From its headwaters in the Rocky Mountains to its confluence with the South Saskatchewan River just east of the Alberta border, the Red Deer River is several hundred miles long. Over that length there are dozens of bridges and other access points, but for the purposes of this book, flyrodders need only concern themselves with two stretches: below Dickson Dam downstream to the Joffre (Secondary Highway 815) Bridge for brown trout; and from the Joffre bridge downstream to Dinosaur Provincial Park for goldeye.

Upstream of the city of Red Deer there are several bridges and road allowances providing access to decent brown trout fishing, but for the most part the river flows through private land. Try the Highway 54 bridge just west of Innisfail. If you continue west on Highway 54 for about eight miles, you'll come to a gravel pit and a small road leading south to the river. There's good holding water both upstream and down, and the braided channels and undercut banks are tailor-made for browns.

A number of bridges cross the river in and downstream of Red Deer. For a long full-day float, put in at one of the city bridges and take out at the Joffre Bridge. One of the things that makes this float interesting is that you never know what you'll catch. Brown trout, whitefish, goldeye, pike, and walleye all inhabit this section, where the river's cool water starts to warm as the current slows and colors-up. Downstream of the Joffre Bridge, the cold-water species disappear altogether as the Red Deer angles south and enters the badlands.

The best places to access the river in this section are at the bridge crossings and provincial parks north and south of Drumheller. However, be forewarned: some of these access points are fairly remote, and you'll have to drive circuitous routes and consult a detailed provincial map to find them. North of Drumheller, try the Secondary Highway 590 bridge west of Big Valley, Dry Island Buffalo Jump Provincial Park, and the Tolman (Secondary Highway 585) Bridge east of Trochu. If you have a boat and can arrange your own vehicle shuttle, two spectacular full-day float trips are possible—one from the former bridge downstream to the provincial park (seven miles) and the other by putting in at the park and taking out at the Tolman Bridge (seven miles).

Downstream of Drumheller, access points include the Willow Creek picnic site, Dorothy (Secondary Highway 848) Bridge, Finnegan Ferry on Secondary Highway 862, and, much farther south, Dinosaur Provincial Park. For more information on any of the above locations, drop by or telephone Just Fishin' at Red Deer and the staff will be glad to help (number and address listed under Guides and Outfitters).

Equipment

Whether you're after brown trout or goldeye, don't show up at the Red Deer with anything lighter than a six-weight rod. The width and volume of the river often necessitate long casts, especially when fishing from shore, and goldeye have a frustrating tendency to feed in the middle of the river. Besides, you never know when a big pike is going to devour your wet fly or streamer, and a three- or four-weight rod is no match for a fish that size. A heavier rod will also make it easier to cast those size 4 Zonkers and sink-tip lines.

Predictably, leader length and tippet size aren't a big deal on the Red Deer. When fishing for brown trout with streamers, I use a short, one- to two-foot leader with a 1X tippet. When you're stripping a thumb-sized fly through the water, don't kid yourself into believing the trout cares what it's attached to. I use pretty much the same rig when fishing wet flies for goldeye. They're not fussy, and the stout tippet is necessary to stand up to their sharp teeth. When the goldeye are feeding on the surface, lengthen the leader a few feet and try a 3X tippet.

I use chest waders on the Red Deer when fishing below the Dickson Dam for browns. Otherwise, I usually wade wet, especially farther downstream in the badlands. The river is predominantly soft-bottomed there; it's rare that I wade out over my knees. As a matter of fact, most of the time I don't venture into the water at all, finding the going easier and safer on the banks. It's not surprising, then, that felt-soled wading boots aren't a requirement on the lower Red Deer, either. A better choice would be a pair of the lightweight, lug-soled, day-hiking shoes so popular nowadays (just be sure that you don't mind dunking them once in awhile).

During the summer, the badlands can be stifling, so bring along some light-colored cotton T-shirts and shorts. Sunscreen and polarized sunglasses are a must, as is a wide-brimmed hat. Nevertheless, even out on the prairies thunderstorms are common, and you should pack rain gear and some warmer clothing. You should also note that even during the hottest weather the mornings and evenings can be surprisingly cool.

Fly Patterns

When it comes to catching goldeye on flies, anything goes. I spent an hour once casting to a rising school of goldeye, repeatedly changing flies, trying to figure out what they *wouldn't* take. No luck. They hit caddis patterns, mayfly patterns, attractor patterns, midge patterns, and patterns that most flyfishers would be embarrassed to possess, let alone fish. At any rate, my favorite dry-fly goldeye pattern continues to be a size 10 yellow-bodied Letort Hopper. That choice has nothing to do with fishing. It's just that hoppers are plentiful in the surrounding badlands, and tying on an imitation of one makes me feel more like part of the *big picture* and less like a blasphemer hurling mud balls at a shrine.

"Fish big, big hoppers and smack them down on the water," says Doug Wood, owner of the Just Fishin' shop in Red Deer. "The goldeye go crazy for them."

Streamers, nymphs, and wet flies are equally effective; I've found that bright materials, such as peacock herl, mylar, and Flashabou, get the goldeyes' attention in turbid water. My favorite subsurface pattern is a yellow-bodied Woolly Worm. The reasoning is twofold: first, goldeye have sharp teeth that quickly mangle flies, and the Woolly Worm is a robust pattern that looks good falling apart; second, Woolly Worms are quick and easy to tie, and going through several in an evening isn't as upsetting as, say, going through the same number of Matuka Sculpins.

As far as the brown trout are concerned, cast big glitzy streamers, such as silver Zonkers, white-bodied Woolly Buggers, and Clouser Minnows in sizes 2 to 6. The Red Deer River browns gorge on whitefish, especially below Dickson Dam, and a brightly-colored streamer is a good whitefish imitation.

I occasionally see browns rising to caddisflies and mayflies below the dam, but not often. River regulars tell me the bulk of their fishing is beneath the surface; the browns seem content to feed on minnows and fry, even when bugs are hatching. Still, it never hurts to bring along a few generic caddis and mayfly patterns in sizes 12 to 18.

Seasons and Tactics

The best time to plan a trip to the lower Red Deer to flyfish for goldeye is from late July to mid-September. The river will be at its clearest then (still colored by trout-stream standards), and chances are good the goldeye will be rising throughout the day, with the heaviest surface activity in the evening. Watch carefully for their dimpling rises, particularly below riffles, in slack water along the banks, in obvious pools, in eddies, and along any foam-flecked seam dividing fast and slow water. If the goldeye aren't rising, fish to them beneath the surface at the same spots, making sure to let the fly sink a few feet before beginning a slow retrieve. Clearly, there's not much skill involved in fishing for goldeye, which makes them a perfect quarry for novice flyfishers and kids. The best advice is that when you catch a goldeye, stay put—they travel in large schools and don't know the meaning of the word spook.

The river between the Dickson Dam and Joffre Bridge opens to fishing in late May, but it's usually dirty then and run-off can last into July. The brown trout will take streamers just as soon as they can spot them. Early in the season is a good time to cast tight to the banks and fish the river much the same way as described in the chapter on the lower Bow River. During the summer and fall, the best way to fish for browns is with weighted streamers and sink-tip lines. Get the fly down deep and strip it back in short, quick jerks. The best places to find browns are deep pools, undercut banks, and around submerged trees and brush. In October these fish get aggressive as they prepare to spawn, and this is a good time to hook a trophy—something in the three- to five-pound range.

Special Regulations

The Red Deer River between the Dickson Dam and Joffre Bridge is open to angling May 20 to February 28. All trout caught in this section must be released. Downstream of the Joffre Bridge the river can be fished year-round, but be aware that most of it freezes over and the goldeye migrate well downstream in the fall and winter months. Goldeye are palatable only if smoked. The daily (and possession) limit is ten fish.

Places to Stay and Eat

Drumheller, Red Deer, and Innisfail all have good numbers of motels and restaurants. Contact the Drumheller Chamber of Commerce (Box 999, Drumheller, Alta., Canada, T0J 0Y0; 403-823-2171). The Red Deer Chamber of Commerce can be reached at 3017 Gates Avenue, Red Deer, Alta., Canada, T4N 5Y6 or by telephone at 403-347-4491.

Provincial and private campgrounds are plentiful in central Alberta. Some of the best are at Gleniffer Lake (Dickson Dam), the Joffre Bridge upstream of the badlands, and at the Tolman Bridge and Dinosaur Provincial Park, north and south of Drumheller, respectively.

Guides and Outfitters

I'm not aware of any commercial fishing guides along the Red Deer River. If you're interested in tackling either the upper or lower sections, the best source of current information is Doug Wood at Just Fishin' in Red Deer (6828 50th Avenue, Red Deer, Alta., Canada, T4N 4E3; 403-340-3474).

Other Attractions

Drumheller's Royal Tyrrell Museum of Paleontology is one of the finest dinosaur museums in the world. Attracting hundreds of thousands of visitors each year, it should be on the "must-see" list of every visitor to southern Alberta. It includes exhibits about earth's geological history, the ice age, the evolution of life, and, of course, the age of dinosaurs. Over thirty complete dinosaur skeletons have been assembled from fossils—many unearthed in the Red Deer River badlands—or reconstructed, including a life-sized Tyrannosaurus rex.

So much for the replicas. At Drumheller's Reptile World, you can see the country's largest live reptile display. If the weather is obliging and you'd rather be outside, consider the thirty-mile Dinosaur Trail loop, a well-marked drive that leaves downtown Drumheller and takes in steeply-cut Horsethief Canyon, the Bleriot Ferry, and several historic coal mines. Farther south, Dinosaur Provincial Park (a United Nations' World Heritage site) features the largest tract of undisturbed badlands in the country.

Index

Other Titles of Interest from Spring Creek Press

An Angler's Guide to Aquatic Insects and Their Imitations
Revised Edition
Rick Hafele and Scott Roederer

Beyond Trout: A Flyfishing Guide
Barry Reynolds and John Berryman
Foreword by John Gierach

Flies for Alaska: A Guide to Buying and Tying
Anthony J. Route

Flyfishing Alaska
Revised Edition
Anthony Route

The Flyrodder's GuideTo Pike!
Video Companion to "Pike on the Fly"
Thomas Smith and Barry Reynolds

Pike On the Fly:
The Flyfishing Guide to Northerns, Tigers, and Muskies
Barry Reynolds and John Berryman
Foreword by Lefty Kreh

Poul Jorgensen's Book of Fly Tying:
A Guide to Flies for All Game Fish
Poul Jorgensen

Woolly Worms and Wombats:
A Sidelong Glance at Flyfishing Down Under
Chris Dawson